Introduction

The "Ninja Dual Zone Air Fryer Cookbook UK 2023" - Perfect for anyone [cooking experience and enjoy a multitude of mouthwatering meals. Thi extensive collection of over 180 recipes that will transform your air frying journey into a truly delightful and budget-friendly dining experience.

One of the standout features of this cookbook is its emphasis on healthier cooking. With the Ninja Dual Zone Air Fryer, you can reduce the amount of fat in your dishes by an impressive 70% compared to traditional cooking methods. This means you and your loved ones can indulge in crispy, delicious meals without worrying about the detrimental effects of excessive cholesterol on your health.

The cookbook covers a wide range of cuisines, ensuring that there's something for everyone's palate. From crispy chicken wings and golden french fries to savory vegetable skewers and delectable desserts, the variety of recipes will keep you inspired and excited to explore the endless possibilities of your Ninja Dual Zone Air Fryer.

What sets this cookbook apart is its thoughtfully designed recipes that are not only delicious but also considerate of your budget. The author understands the importance of providing cost-effective meal options without compromising on taste or quality. With these recipes, you can enjoy incredible dishes without breaking the bank, making it a perfect choice for individuals or families looking to save money while still savoring fantastic meals.

Whether you're a seasoned air frying enthusiast or just starting your culinary journey, the "Ninja Dual Zone Air Fryer Cookbook UK 2023" offers clear and easy-to-follow instructions that will empower you to create restaurant-quality dishes in the comfort of your own kitchen. Get ready to embark on a culinary adventure and savor crispy, delicious creations that will impress your taste buds and nourish your body.

We are dedicated to providing you with exceptional reading materials while also considering the environmental impact of our operations. By opting for black and white printing, we are taking a step towards reducing the toxicity associated with color inks and making a positive contribution to preserving our planet for future generations.
We understand that this change may have caused some small issues that have affected your reading experience. We genuinely apologize for any inconveniences caused. Your feedback is incredibly valuable to us, as it provides us with the opportunity to learn and grow. We appreciate your understanding and patience as we work towards improving our future publications.

Once again, we extend our sincerest thanks for your support and understanding. Thank you for being a part of our journey, and we look forward to serving you with even better products in the future.

What is the Ninja Foodi Dual Zone Air Fryer?

The Ninja Foodi Dual Zone Air Fryer is a versatile kitchen appliance that combines the functions of an air fryer, a countertop oven, and a dehydrator. It is a new model of air fryer, first introduced in 2020, this is designed to provide a convenient and efficient way to cook a wide variety of meals with less oil and faster cooking times.

The Dual Zone feature of the Ninja Foodi Air Fryer allows you to independently control and cook different foods simultaneously in two separate cooking zones. This means you can air fry crispy chicken wings in one zone while baking a delicious dessert in the other, all at the same time. The separate temperature controls and cooking timers for each zone ensure that your dishes are perfectly cooked without any flavor transfer between the zones.

The air frying function of the Ninja Foodi Dual Zone Air Fryer offers a healthier alternative to deep frying. By using superheated air, it can create a crispy and golden exterior on your favorite foods while reducing the amount of oil needed by up to 75%. This not only helps to lower the fat content in your meals but also makes cleanup easier compared to traditional deep frying methods.

In addition to air frying, the Ninja Foodi Dual Zone Air Fryer can also be used as a countertop oven. It features a spacious cooking cavity that can accommodate a variety of dishes, from pizzas and casseroles to roasted vegetables and baked goods. With the ability to bake, roast, and broil, you can achieve a wide range of cooking results with just one appliance.

Furthermore, the Ninja Foodi Dual Zone Air Fryer has a built-in dehydrator function. This allows you to easily transform fresh fruits, vegetables, and meats into flavorful dried snacks or ingredients for your favorite recipes. The dehydrator function helps to preserve the natural flavors and nutrients in the food while extending its shelf life.

Overall, the Ninja Foodi Dual Zone Air Fryer is a versatile and innovative kitchen appliance that offers multiple cooking functions in one. With its dual zone capability, air frying technology, countertop oven features, and dehydrator function, it provides a convenient and efficient way to prepare a wide variety of meals, all while promoting healthier cooking methods.

What makes Ninja Dual Zone Air Fryer different?

The Ninja Dual Zone Air Fryer stands out from other air fryers on the market due to its unique dual zone feature. This innovative design allows you to independently control and cook different foods simultaneously in two separate cooking zones within the same appliance.

The ability to cook in two zones simultaneously provides several advantages. First, it increases cooking versatility and efficiency. You can air fry crispy chicken wings in one zone while baking a dessert or roasting vegetables in the other zone, all at the same time. This saves you time and effort in the kitchen, allowing you to prepare complete meals with different components simultaneously.

The dual zone feature also eliminates flavor transfer between the two cooking zones. This means you can cook savory and sweet dishes at the same time without worrying about the flavors blending together. You can achieve optimal results for each dish without compromising taste or texture.

Easy to Clean: The cooking basket and crisper plate are both non-stick and dishwasher safe, making cleanup quick and effortless.

Additionally, the Ninja Dual Zone Air Fryer offers independent temperature and cooking time controls for each zone. This allows you to customize the cooking settings according to the specific requirements of each food item. For example, you can set a higher temperature and longer cooking time for crispy fried chicken in one zone, while simultaneously setting a lower temperature and shorter cooking time for delicate baked goods in the other zone. The precise control over each zone ensures that each dish is cooked to perfection.

Smart Finish Feature: This feature ensures that both zones finish cooking at the same time, making meal planning and prep much easier. The device also includes a digital timer and temperature control, allowing users to adjust the cook ing time and temperature to suit their specific needs

The versatility of the Ninja Dual Zone Air Fryer extends beyond air frying. It also functions as a countertop oven, providing additional cooking options such as baking, roasting, and broiling. With this appliance, you can easily prepare a wide variety of meals, from appetizers and main courses to desserts, all in one compact unit.

A Beginner's Guide

6 Ways to cook – Max Crisp, Roast, Air Fry, Reheat, Dehydrate and Bake.

When it comes to cooking, timing is everything. The Ninja Foodi Dual Zone Air Fryer does the thinking and timing for you. Cook 2 different foods with different temperatures, times and settings in 2 separate cooking drawers – and have both ready to serve at exactly the same time using the SYNC feature! More people to feed? MATCH settings across both zones to make double the amount of food in the same amount of time!

MATCH

Cooking for extra guests or feeding the whole family? Use the Match feature to double your serving size, with the same cooking program and time in both drawers.

Cook the same food in both zones to make twice the amount of food in the same amount of time! Or easily cook two different foods with the same cooking instructions.

Just cooking for yourself? No problem – you can cook in a single drawer. Each non-stick, dishwasher-safe 3.8L drawer fits up to 1kg of fries.

SYNC

Want to cook two different foods using different times, temperatures and programs? Use different settings in each drawer with the Sync feature – both are ready to serve at the same time!

Want to Roast in one drawer and Air Fry in the other? No problem! Different cooking times for fish fingers and fries? Both finish cooking at the same time, so you can enjoy freshly-cooked mains and sides together – no need to use different appliances or let your side go cold while your main finishes cooking!

Whether it's chicken breasts and fluffy roast potatoes, baked salmon and Mediterranean vegetables or juicy beef burgers and golden chips, your perfect pairing is just moments away.

Cooking for two different dietary requirements? Cater for everyone by cooking vegetarian food in one drawer and meat in the other.

AIR FRY   **MAX CRISP**   **ROAST**   **BAKE**   **DEHYDRATE**   **REHEAT**

More Than an Air Fryer

Up to 75% faster than fan ovens, quickly and easily create a delicious variety of meals that the whole family will love.

AIR FRY– Up 70% less fat than traditional frying methods. Enjoy guilt-free fried favourites using little to no oil. From delicious chicken wings, fishcakes, burgers and sausages to chunky chips. Air frying evenly circulates super-hot air around food to remove excess moisture and give it a delicious golden finish.

MAX CRISP– Cook from frozen to crispy in minutes. Temperatures of 240°C evenly cook and crisp your favourite frozen foods. From breaded scampi and chicken nuggets to golden French fries, onion rings and more. Perfect for quick, delicious dinners.

ROAST – Not just for Sundays, enjoy your favourite roast meat, fish and vegetables any day of the week. From salmon fillets, golden chicken breasts and roast pork chops with crispy crackling to fluffy roast potatoes, balsamic-roasted tomatoes and sweet potato hash.

DEHYDRATE – Create delicious dried fruit snacks, from apple to mango, banana to pineapple. Enjoy homemade vegetable crisps, beef jerky, and even make your own dried herbs.

BAKE – Easily cook pasta bakes, fish pies and flaky fish with crispy toppings, or enjoy freshly-baked bread and homemade sweet treats, from muffins and brownies to cakes and cookies.

REHEAT – Restore leftovers to that delicious fresh-out-of-the-oven finish, perfect for reviving leftover pizza, quiche, spring rolls and more.

Variable temperature controls let you make every snack and meal just how you like it. The innovative Auto-Adjust Fan automatically changes speeds based on the cooking function selected.

The easy-to-use digital control panel with a countdown timer makes it easy to see how much cooking time is left.

Washing up is easy thanks to non-stick, dishwasher-safe parts.

Troubleshooting Guide

How do I adjust the temperature or time while using a single zone?	Select the active zone, then use the TEMP arrows to adjust the temperature or the TIME arrows to adjust the time.
How do I adjust the temperature or time while using dual zones?	Select the desired zone, then use the TEMP arrows to adjust the temperature or the TIME arrows to adjust the time.
Does the unit need to pre-heat?	The unit does not need to be pre-heated.
Can I cook different foods in each zone and not worry about cross contamination?	Yes, both zones are self-contained with separate heating elements and fans.
How do I pause the countdown?	The countdown timer will pause automatically when you remove the drawers from the unit. Reinsert drawer within 2 minutes to resume cooking or the unit will automatically switch off.
How do I stop one zone when using both zones?	To stop one zone, first press the zone button then press START/STOP. To stop both zones simply press the START/STOP button.
Is the drawer safe to put on my worktop?	The drawer will heat up during cooking. Use caution when handling, and place on heat resistant surfaces only.
When should I use the crisper plate?	Use the crisper plate when you want food to come out crispy. The plate elevates the food in the drawer so that air can flow under and around it to cook ingredients evenly.
Why didn't my food cook fully?	Make sure the drawer is fully inserted during cooking. For consistent browning, make sure ingredients are arranged in an even layer on the bottom of the drawer with no overlapping. Shake drawer to toss ingredients for even crispiness. Cook temperature and time can be adjusted at any time during cooking. Simply use the TEMP arrows to adjust the temperature or the TIME arrows to adjust the time.
Why is my food burned?	For best results, check progress throughout cooking and remove food when desired level of brownness has been achieved. Remove food immediately after the cook time is complete to avoid overcooking.
Why do some ingredients blow around when air frying?	Occasionally, the fan from the air fryer will blow lightweight foods around. Use wooden cocktail sticks to secure loose lightweight food, like the top slice of bread on a sandwich.
Can I air fry wet, battered ingredients?	Yes, but use the proper breading technique. It is important to coat foods first with flour, then with egg, and then with bread crumbs. Press breading firmly onto the battered ingredients, so crumbs won't be blown off by the fan.
Why is the unit beeping?	The food is done cooking or indicates that the other zone started cooking.
Why did the display screen go black?	The unit is in standby mode. Press the power button to turn it back on.
What is the temperature range of the unit?	The temperature ranges from 40°C (for Dehydrate) to 240°C (for Max Crisp). Roast, Air Fry, Reheat, and Bake only goes up to 210°C.
What is Max Crisp?	Max Crisp Technology provides hotter, faster, and crispier results for all your favorite prepackaged frozen foods. Max Crisp cooks at 240°C. For best results, reduce cook times and shake food often.
How many cooking functions are included with the unit?	The unit has 6 different cooking functions: Max Crisp, Air Fry, Dehydrate, Roast, Bake, and Reheat
How much food can I cook in each drawer?	Each 3.8L cooking drawer fits up to 1kg of fries or a whole 1.6kg chicken.

CLEANING & MAINTENANCE:

The unit should be cleaned thoroughly after every use. Unplug the unit from the plug socket and wait until the unit is fully cooled before cleaning.

Main Unit: To clean the main unit and the control panel, wipe them clean with a damp cloth. NEVER immerse the main unit in water or any other liquid. NEVER clean the main unit in a dishwasher.

Drawers and Crisper Plates: These can be washed in the dishwasher or by hand. If handwashed Air-dry or towel-dry all parts after use. To extend the life of the drawers, recommend hand-washing them.

If food residue is stuck on the crisper plates or drawers, place them in a sink filled with warm, soapy water and allow to soak.

1. We use the average capacity of Ninja Dual Zone Air Fryer models to write our recipes. Therefore, if one of the cooking instructions is for one zone but it doesn't fit in a single zone of your air fryer, divide it and cook it on two zones, and vice versa. The temperature and time still follow our provided formulas.

2. The MATCH button is frequently used to duplicate settings across both zones. However, don't forget about the SYNC button when you want to cook two separate dishes and serve them simultaneously.

Helpful Cooking Tips

1. For consistent browning, make sure ingredients are arranged in an even layer on the bottom of the drawer with no overlapping. If ingredients are overlapping, make sure to shake them halfway through the set cook time.

2. Cook temperature and time can be adjusted at any time during cooking. Simply select the zone you want to adjust, then press the TEMP arrows to adjust the temperature or the TIME arrows to adjust the time.

3. To convert recipes from your conventional oven, reduce the temperature by 10°C. Check food frequently to avoid overcooking.

4. Occasionally, the fan from the air fryer will blow lightweight foods around. To alleviate this, secure foods (like the top slice of bread on a sandwich) with cocktail sticks.

5. The crisper plates elevate ingredients in the drawers so air can circulate under and around ingredients for even, crisp results.

6. After selecting a cooking function, you can press the START/STOP button to begin cooking immediately. The unit will run at the default temperature and time.

7. For best results with fresh vegetables and potatoes, use at least 1 tablespoon of oil. Add more oil as desired to achieve the preferred level of crispiness.

8. For best results, check progress throughout cooking and remove food when desired level of brownness has been achieved. We recommend using an instant-read thermometer to monitor the internal temperature of meat & fish. After the cook time is complete, remove food immediately to avoid overcooking.

9. For best results, remove food immediately after the cook time is complete to avoid overcooking.

Table of Content

All About Ninja Dual Zone Air Fryer

I. Introductions

II. What is the Ninja Foodi Dual Zone Air Fryer?

III. What makes Ninja Dual Zone Air Fryer different?

IV. Beginner's Guide

V. More Than an Air Fryer

VI. Troubleshooting Guide

VII. Helpful Cooking Tips

Chapter 1: Breakfasts

1	Morning Egg Rolls
1	Pepper Egg Cups
2	Hearty Cheddar Biscuits
2	Cheese & Chive Scones
3	Cheese Sandwich
3	Banana Muffins
4	Hash Browns
4	Burritos
5	Morning Quiche
5	Samosas
6	Breakfast Potatoes
6	Cornbread
7	Turkey Ham Muffin
7	Sausage Egg Cup
8	Pizza Eggs
8	Bacon, Broccoli & Cheese Bread Pudding
9	Cheese & Ham Toasted Sandwiches
9	Bunless Turkey Burgers
10	Cinnamon-Raisin Bagels
10	Cajun Breakfast Sausage
11	English Muffins
11	Spinach Omelet
12	Asparagus and Bell Pepper Strata
12	Pancake Cake
13	Egg Tarts
13	Red Pepper & Feta Frittata
14	Fried Chicken Wings with Waffles
15	Cinnamon Rolls

Chapter 2: Everyday Favourites & Sides

16	Air Fried Broccoli
16	Scalloped Veggie Mix
17	Indian-Style Sweet Potato Fries
17	Bacon Pinwheels
18	Glazed Sweet Potato Bites
18	Cheese-Walnut Stuffed Mushrooms
19	Gold Artichoke Hearts
19	Fried Brussels Sprouts
20	Potato with Creamy Cheese
20	Balsamic Brussels Sprouts
21	Garlic Herb Radishes
21	Crispy Garlic Sliced Aubergine

Table of Content

22 Dijon Roast Cabbage
22 Crispy Chickpeas
23 Fried Courgette Salad
23 Ricotta Potatoes
24 Mushrooms with Goat Cheese
24 Green Tomato Salad
25 Lush Vegetable Salad
25 Corn & Coriander Salad
26 Traditional Queso Fundido
26 Beetroot Salad with Lemon Vinaigrette
27 Purple Potato Chips with Rosemary
27 Baked Cheese Sandwich
28 Butter & Garlic Fried Cabbage
28 Lebanese Baba Ghanoush
29 Cheesy Baked Grits
29 Beery & Crunchy Onion Rings
30 Air Fried Courgette Sticks
30 Easy Croutons
31 Buffalo Cauliflower with Blue Cheese
32 Dinner Rolls
33 Crispy Lemon Artichoke Hearts

Chapter 3: Family's Favorites Dishes

34 Cheddar Quiche
34 Air Fryer Chicken Wings
35 BBQ Chicken & Chips
35 Cheesy Quesadillas with Salsa
36 Fish & Vegetable Tacos
36 Pork Stuffing Meatballs
37 Fried Green Tomatoes
37 Chinese-Inspired Spareribs
38 Cajun Shrimp
38 Veggie Tuna Melts
39 Coconut Chicken Tenders
39 Steak & Vegetable Kebabs
40 Frittata
40 Spicy Chicken Tenders

Chapter 4: Poultry

41 Easy Chicken Nachos
41 Turkey Meatloaf
42 African Merguez Meatballs
42 Honey-Glazed Chicken Thighs
43 Easy Cajun Chicken Drumsticks
43 Chicken Pesto Pizzas
44 Ginger Turmeric Chicken Thighs
44 Lemon Thyme Roasted Chicken
45 Spice-Rubbed Chicken Thighs
45 Pickle Brined Fried Chicken
46 Teriyaki Chicken Legs
46 French Garlic Chicken
47 Cheese-Encrusted Chicken Tenderloins with Peanuts
47 Bacon-Wrapped Chicken Breasts Rolls
48 Chicken & Broccoli Casserole
48 Chicken with Masala Fries
49 Chicken Fajitas & Spicy Roast Potatoes Bruschetta Chicken
50 Golden Chicken Cutlets
51 Chicken Croquettes with Creole Sauce
52 Stuffed Turkey Roulade
53 Chicken, Courgette, & Spinach Salad
54 Barbecued Chicken with Creamy
55 Coleslaw

Table of Content

Chapter 5: Beef, Pork, & Lamb

56	*Chorizo & Beef Burger*
56	*Italian Sausage & Cheese Meatballs*
57	*Fried Pork & Sweet Potato Fries*
57	*Bacon Wrapped Pork Chops & Quinoa*
58	*Cajun Bacon Pork Loin Fillet*
58	*Lemon Pork with Marjoram*
59	*Reuben Beef Rolls with Thousand Island Sauce*
59	*Beef & Spinach Rolls*
60	*Pork Medallions with Endive Salad*
60	*Cheese Crusted Chops*
61	*Bacon Wrapped Pork with Apple Gravy*
61	*Italian Sausage Links*
62	*Meat & Rice Stuffed Peppers*
62	*Spicy Rump Steak*
63	*Sumptuous Pizza Tortilla Rolls*
63	*Bacon-Wrapped Cheese Pork*
64	*Southern Chili*
64	*Bacon & Cheese Stuffed Pork Chops*
65	*Beef Mince Taco Rolls*
65	*Pork Kebab with Yogurt Sauce*
66	*Marinated Steak Tips with Mushrooms*
66	*Cheese Pork Chop*
67	*Chicken Fried Steak with Cream Gravy*
68	*Bean & Beef Meatball Taco Pizza*
69	*Roast Beef with Horseradish Cream*

Chapter 6: Fish & Seafood

70	*Salmon on Bed of Fennel & Carrot*
70	*Garlic Lemon Scallops*
71	*Crispy Fish Sticks*
71	*Sole & Cauliflower Fritters*
72	*Prawn Dejonghe Skewers*
72	*Butter-Wine Baked Salmon*
73	*Foil-Packet Lobster Tail*
73	*Scallops with Asparagus and Peas*
74	*Paprika Prawns*
74	*Roasted Cod with Lemon-Garlic Potatoes*
75	*Browned Prawns Patties*
75	*Lemon Pepper Prawns*
76	*Nutty Prawns with Amaretto Glazet*
76	*Crab-Stuffed Avocado Boats*
77	*Garlic Butter Prawns Scampi*
77	*Moroccan Spiced Halibut with Chickpea Salad*
78	*Fish Cakes*
78	*Thai Fishcakes*
79	*Cooked Tuna with Lemongrass*
79	*Miso Salmon*
80	*Breaded Prawns Tacos*
81	*Thai Prawn Skewers with Peanut Dipping Sauce*

Chapter 7: Appetizers & Snacks

82	*Spring Rolls*
82	*Prawn Toast*
83	*Baked Spanakopita Dip*
83	*Parmesan French Fries*

Table of Content

- 84   *Mexican Jalapeno Poppers*
- 84   *Crab Cake Poppers*
- 85   *Fried Halloumi Cheese*
- 85   *Cauliflower Gnocchi*
- 86   *Pickle Chips*
- 86   *Sweet Potato Fries with Mayonnaise*
- 87   *Crispy Chilli Chickpeas*
- 87   *Tangy Fried Pickle Spears*
- 88   *Chilli-Brined Fried Calamari*
- 88   *Roasted Grape Dip*
- 89   *Air Fried Pot Stickers*
- 89   *Crispy Mozzarella Sticks*
- 90   *Veggie Shrimp Toast*
- 90   *Garlic-Parmesan Croutons*
- 91   *Easy Spiced Nuts*
- 91   *Crispy Green Tomatoes with*
- 92   *Horseradish*
- 92   *Lemony Pear Chips*
- 93   *Sea Salt Potato Crisps*
- 94   *Crispy Filo Artichoke Triangles Stuffed Bell Peppers*

Chapter 8: Vegetarian Mains

- 95   *Quiche-Stuffed Peppers*
- 95   *Russet Potato Gratin*
- 96   *Pesto Spinach Flatbread*
- 96   *Stuffed Portobellos*
- 97   *Cheese Stuffed Peppers*
- 97   *Mediterranean Air Fried Veggies*
- 98   *Air-fried Radishes*
- 98   *Stuffed Tomatoes*
- 99   *Curly Fries*
- 99   *Herb and Lemon Cauliflowe*
- 100   *Cheesy Cabbage Wedges*
- 100   *Cauliflower Rice-Stuffed Peppers*
- 101   *Zucchini With Stuffing*
- 101   *Mixed Air Fry Veggies*
- 102   *Chickpea Fritters*
- 102   *Croutons*
- 103   *Buffalo Seitan With Crispy Zucchini Noodles*
- 104   *Super Vegetable Burger*

Chapter 9: Desserts

- 105   *Baked Brazilian Pineapple*
- 105   *Mini Cheesecake*
- 106   *Gingerbread*
- 106   *White Chocolate Cookies*
- 107   *Pumpkin Pudding with Vanilla Wafers*
- 107   *Blueberry Cheesecake Pies*
- 108   *Pumpkin Cookie with Cream Cheese Frosting*
- 109   *Chocolate Donuts*
- 109   *Almond Butter Cookies*
- 110   *Apple Dutch Baby*
- 110   *Ricotta Lemon Poppy Seed Cake*
- 111   *Jelly Doughnuts*

Morning Egg Rolls

Serves: 2 | Prep & Cook time: 22 Min

- 4 large eggs
- 2 tablespoons milk
- 4 small flour tortillas
- 50g grated cheddar cheese
- 1/4 red bell pepper, diced
- 2 spring onions, finely chopped
- Salt and pepper to taste.

DIRECTIONS:

1. In a bowl, whisk together the eggs and milk until well combined.
2. Add the grated cheddar cheese, diced red bell pepper, chopped spring onions, salt, and pepper to the egg mixture. Stir well to incorporate all the ingredients.
3. Place a flour tortilla on a clean surface or cutting board. Spoon a quarter of the egg mixture onto one side of the tortilla.
4. Roll the tortilla tightly, tucking in the sides as you go, to form an egg roll. Repeat this process for the remaining tortillas and egg mixture.
5. Place the egg rolls in Zone 1 of the Ninja Dual Zone Air Fryer, ensuring they are arranged in a single layer.
6. Select Zone 1, choose the AIR FRY program, and set the temperature to 180°C. Set the time to 10-12 minutes.
7. Press the START/STOP button to begin cooking.
8. Check the egg rolls after 10 minutes to see if they are golden brown and crispy. If not, cook for an additional 1-2 minutes.
9. Once cooked, carefully remove the egg rolls from the air fryer and let them cool for a few minutes.
10. Serve the **Morning Egg Rolls** warm with your preferred dipping sauce or enjoy them on their own.

Pepper Egg Cups

Serves: 2 | Prep & Cook time: 22 Min

- 4 medium eggs
- 2 large bell peppers (red, yellow, or green)
- 60g grated cheddar cheese
- 2 spring onions, finely chopped
- Fresh herbs (such as parsley or chives) for garnish
- Salt and pepper to taste.

DIRECTIONS:

1. Cut the top off each bell pepper and remove the seeds and membranes. Trim the bottoms slightly, if needed, to help them stand upright in Zone 1 of the air fryer.
2. In a small bowl, crack the eggs and whisk them together. Add the grated cheddar cheese, chopped spring onions, salt, and pepper. Mix well.
3. Place the bell peppers upright in Zone 1 of the air fryer, ensuring they are stable and won't tip over.
4. Carefully pour the egg mixture into each pepper, dividing it equally.
5. Select Zone 1 on the Ninja Dual Zone Air Fryer, choose the BAKE program, and set the temperature to 180°C. Set the time to 10-12 minutes (or until the eggs are set and the peppers have softened slightly).
6. Press the START/STOP button to begin cooking.
7. Once cooked, carefully remove the **pepper egg cups** from the air fryer using oven mitts or tongs.
8. Garnish with fresh herbs and serve hot.

Chapter 1: Breakfasts

Hearty Cheddar Biscuits

Serves: 8 biscuit | Prep & Cook time: 25 Min

- 225g self-raising flour
- 150ml milk
- 1 teaspoon baking powder
- 50g unsalted butter, cold and cubed
- 100g grated cheddar cheese
- 1/2 teaspoon salt
- 1 tablespoon chopped fresh chives or spring onions (optional)
- 1 tablespoon melted butter, for brushing (optional)

DIRECTIONS:

1. In a large bowl, mix together the self-raising flour, baking powder, and salt.
2. Add the cold, cubed butter to the flour mixture. Use your fingers to rub the butter into the flour until the mixture resembles coarse breadcrumbs.
3. Stir in the grated cheddar cheese and chopped fresh chives or spring onions, if using.
4. Gradually pour in the milk while stirring the mixture. Mix until the dough comes together. Be careful not to overmix.
5. Turn the dough out onto a floured surface and gently knead it a few times until it becomes smooth.
6. Roll out the dough to a thickness of about 2cm.
7. Use a round biscuit cutter to cut out 8 biscuits from the dough.
8. Place the biscuits in Zone 1 of the Air Fryer.
9. Select Zone 1, choose the BAKE program, and set the temperature to 180°C. Set the time to 10 minutes. Press START/STOP to begin cooking.
10. After 8 minutes of cooking time, open the drawer and brush the tops of the biscuits with melted butter, if desired. This step will give them a golden, glossy finish.
11. Close the drawer and continue cooking for the remaining time.
12. When the cooking time is complete, remove the drawer from the Air Fryer.
13. Allow the biscuits to cool slightly before serving.
14. Serve the **Hearty Cheddar Biscuits** warm as a delightful accompaniment to soups, stews, or enjoyed on their own as a tasty snack.

Cheese & Chive Scones

Serves: 8 | Prep & Cook time: 25 Min

- 1 large egg
- 270g plain flour
- 30g Parmesan or vegetarian equivalent
- 40g mature cheddar, grated
- 100g butter, cut into cubes, softened
- 60g crème fraiche
- 1 tablespoon fresh chives, finely chopped
- 1 teaspoon baking powder
- 1/2 teaspoon salt
- Milk for brushing

DIRECTIONS:

1. In a large bowl, add flour, baking powder, salt, chives, cheddar and Parmesan. Mix well and then add egg, softened butter and crème fraiche. Use your fingers to combine mixture together, then place on a clean lightly floured surface, knead lightly until all loose flour has been worked into the dough. Don't overwork the dough because scones should be flaky and buttery.
2. Roll out the dough approximately 3cm thick. Using a 6cm biscuit cutter cut out scones, re-roll left over dough and cut again to make 8 scones.
3. Brush top of scones with milk.
4. Insert crisper plates into both drawers. Spray with oil, add 4 scones into each drawer. Select zone 1, select BAKE, set temperature to 170°C and set time to 10 minutes. Select MATCH. Press START/STOP to begin.
5. When cooking is complete, remove the **scones** and allow to cool down. Serve with butter, chutney.

Cheese Sandwich

Serves: 2 | Prep & Cook time: 25 Min

- 2 large eggs
- 4 slices of bread (white, brown, or wholemeal)
- 4 slices of cooked bacon or ham
- 4 slices of cheddar cheese
- Butter or cooking spray for greasing.

DIRECTIONS:

1. Grease the bottom of Zone 1 of the air fryer with butter or cooking spray.
2. Place two slices of bread in Zone 1 of the Ninja Dual Zone Air Fryer, side by side.
3. Layer each slice of bread with a slice of cheddar cheese and a slice of cooked bacon or ham.
4. Create a small well in the center of each sandwich by gently pressing down the bread in the middle.
5. Crack one egg into each well, being careful not to break the yolks.
6. Place the remaining two slices of bread on top of each sandwich to complete the sandwiches.
7. Close the air fryer and make sure it is securely in place.
8. Select Zone 1, choose the BAKE program, and set the temperature to 180°C. Set the time to 8-10 minutes. Press the START/STOP button to begin cooking.
9. Check the sandwiches after 8 minutes to see if the eggs are cooked to your desired doneness. If you prefer runny yolks, cook for a shorter time, and for fully cooked yolks, cook for a longer time.
10. Once cooked, carefully remove the **Cheese Sandwiches** from the air fryer.
11. Allow the sandwiches to cool for a minute or two before serving.

Banana Muffins

Serves: 4 | Prep & Cook time: 30 Min

- 1 large egg
- 120g all-purpose flour
- 2 ripe bananas, mashed
- 60g unsalted butter, melted
- 80g granulated sugar
- 1 teaspoon baking powder
- 1/2 teaspoon baking soda
- 1/4 teaspoon salt
- 60ml milk
- 1/2 teaspoon vanilla extract.

DIRECTIONS:

1. In a mixing bowl, combine the mashed bananas, melted butter, granulated sugar, and egg. Mix well until well combined.
2. In a separate bowl, whisk together the flour, baking powder, baking soda, and salt.
3. Gradually add the dry ingredient mixture to the banana mixture, alternating with the milk. Stir until just combined. Avoid overmixing. Stir in the vanilla extract.
4. Place paper liners in the muffin cups or grease the cups with butter or oil.
5. Divide the muffin batter evenly among the prepared muffin cups, filling each about two-thirds full.
6. Place the muffin cups in Zone 1 of the Ninja Dual Zone Air Fryer.
7. Select Zone 1, choose the BAKE program, and set the temperature to 180°C. Set the time to 12-15 minutes. Press the START/STOP button to begin cooking.
8. Check the muffins after 12 minutes with a toothpick or skewer inserted into the center. If it comes out clean or with a few crumbs, the muffins are ready. If not, continue cooking for a few more minutes.
9. Once cooked, carefully remove the muffins from the air fryer and let them cool in the **muffin** cups for a few minutes.
10. Transfer the muffins to a wire rack to cool completely.

Hash Browns

Serves: 2 | Prep & Cook time: 30 Min

- 400g potatoes, peeled and grated
- 1 tablespoon plain flour
- 1 small onion, grated
- 1/4 teaspoon black pepper
- 1/2 teaspoon salt
- Cooking oil spray

DIRECTIONS:

1. Preheat the Ninja Dual Zone Air Fryer to 200°C (Zone 1).
2. In a bowl, combine the grated potatoes, grated onion, plain flour, salt, and black pepper. Mix well to combine.
3. Spray Zone 1 with cooking oil spray.
4. Take a handful of the potato mixture and shape it into a hash brown patty. Place it in Zone 1 of the air fryer. Repeat with the remaining mixture, making sure to leave some space between the patties.
5. Spray the hash browns with cooking oil spray.
6. Select Zone 1 on the Ninja Dual Zone Air Fryer, choose the AIR FRY program, and set the temperature to 200°C. Set the time to 15 minutes.
7. Press the START/STOP button to begin cooking.
8. After 10 minutes, carefully flip the hash browns and air fry for an additional 5 minutes or until they are golden brown and crispy.
9. Once cooked, remove the **hash browns** from the air fryer and let them cool slightly before serving.

Burritos

Serves: 2 | Prep & Cook time: 20 Min

- 4 large eggs
- 50g cheddar cheese, grated
- 50g cooked bacon or sausage, chopped
- 1/2 green bell pepper, diced
- 1/2 red onion, diced
- 2 large flour tortillas
- Salt and pepper, to taste
- Cooking oil spray

DIRECTIONS:

1. Preheat the Ninja Dual Zone Air Fryer to 180°C (both Zone).
2. In a bowl, whisk the eggs until well beaten. Season with salt and pepper.
3. Spray two Zone with cooking oil spray. Pour the beaten eggs into Zone 1 and Choose AIR FRY to 180°C for 5 minutes (or until they are softly scrambled, stirring occasionally). Press the START/STOP button.
4. In the Zone 2, add the diced bell pepper and onion. Choose ROAST to 180°C for 3-4 minutes or until they are slightly softened. Press the START/STOP button.
5. Once the eggs are cooked, transfer them to a plate and set aside.
6. Remove the cooked bell pepper and onion from Zone 2 and set aside.
7. Lay out the flour tortillas and divide the scrambled eggs, cooked bell pepper, onion, grated cheese, and chopped bacon or sausage evenly between the two tortillas.
8. Fold the sides of the tortillas over the filling, then roll them up tightly to form burritos.
9. Spray Zone 1 with cooking oil spray again. Place the burritos in Zone 1, seam-side down. Select Zone 1, Choose AIR FRY program, set the temperature to 180°C for 5 minutes or until they are crispy and golden. Press the START/STOP button.
10. Once cooked, remove the **burritos** from the air fryer and let them cool slightly before serving.

Morning Quiche

Serves: 2 | Prep & Cook time: 30 Min

- 4 large eggs
- 4 slices of bacon, cooked and crumbled
- 1/2 small onion, finely chopped
- 1/2 red bell pepper, diced
- 50g cheddar cheese, grated
- 50ml milk
- Salt and pepper to taste
- Cooking oil spray.

DIRECTIONS:

1. Spray Zone 1 with cooking oil spray.
2. In a bowl, beat the eggs and milk together. Season with salt and pepper.
3. In another bowl, combine the cooked bacon, chopped onion, and diced red bell pepper.
4. Divide the bacon and vegetable mixture evenly into two individual ramekins.
5. Pour the egg mixture over the bacon and vegetables in each ramekin. Top with grated cheddar cheese.
6. Place the ramekins in Zone 1 of the air fryer. Make sure they are stable and won't tip over.
7. Select Zone 1, choose the AIR FRY program, and set the temperature to 180°C. Set the time to 15 minutes (or until the eggs are set and the cheese is melted and golden brown).
8. Once cooked, carefully remove the quiches from the air fryer using oven mitts or tongs.
9. Allow the quiches to cool for a few minutes before serving.
10. Serve the **Breakfast Quiche** warm as a delicious and filling breakfast. The combination of bacon, vegetables, and cheese creates a flavorful and satisfying dish. Enjoy!

Samosas

Serves: 2 | Prep & Cook time: 20 Min

- 2 medium potatoes, boiled and mashed
- 1 green chili, finely chopped
- 1 small onion, finely chopped
- 1/2 teaspoon cumin seeds
- 1/2 teaspoon garam masala
- 50g peas
- 1/2 teaspoon turmeric powder
- 1/2 teaspoon red chili powder
- 2 sheets of ready-made puff pastry, thawed
- Salt to taste.

DIRECTIONS:

1. In a pan, heat a small amount of oil and add cumin seeds. Once they start to sizzle, add the chopped onion and green chili. Sauté until the onion turns golden brown.
2. Add the peas, garam masala, turmeric powder, red chili powder, and salt to the pan. Cook for a few minutes until the peas are tender.
3. Add the mashed potatoes to the pan and mix well with the spice mixture. Cook for another 2-3 minutes. Remove from heat and let the filling cool.
4. Cut each sheet of puff pastry into 4 equal-sized squares.
5. Take one square of puff pastry and place a spoonful of the potato filling in the center. Fold the pastry diagonally to form a triangle and seal the edges by pressing with a fork. Repeat with the remaining squares and filling.
6. Spray Zone 1 with cooking oil spray.
7. Place the samosas in Zone 1 of the air fryer. Select Zone 1, choose the AIR FRY program, and set the temperature to 180°C. Set the time to 15 minutes (or until they turn golden brown and crispy).
8. Press the START/STOP button to begin cooking.
9. Once cooked, carefully remove the **samosas** from the air fryer using oven mitts or tongs.

Serve the Breakfast Samosas warm as a delightful and flavorful breakfast. You can enjoy them as is or pair them with your favorite chutney or dip

Breakfast Potatoes

Serves: 2 | Prep & Cook time: 35 Min

- 400g potatoes, peeled and diced into small cubes
- 2 tablespoons olive oil
- 1 teaspoon paprika
- 1/2 teaspoon garlic powder
- 1/2 teaspoon onion powder
- 1/2 teaspoon dried thyme
- Salt and pepper to taste
- Fresh parsley, chopped (optional, for garnish)

DIRECTIONS:

1. In a mixing bowl, combine the diced potatoes, olive oil, paprika, garlic powder, onion powder, dried thyme, salt, and pepper. Toss well to evenly coat the potatoes with the seasonings.
2. Place the seasoned potatoes in Zone 1 of the Ninja Dual Zone Air Fryer.
3. Select Zone 1, choose the AIR FRY program, and set the temperature to 180°C. Set the time to 20-25 minutes.
4. Press the START/STOP button to begin cooking.
5. Shake the potatoes in Zone 1 every 5-10 minutes to ensure even cooking and browning.
6. Check the potatoes after 20 minutes to see if they are golden brown and crispy. If not, cook for an additional 5 minutes.
7. Once cooked, carefully remove the **potatoes** from the air fryer and transfer them to a serving dish.
8. Garnish with fresh chopped parsley, if desired.

Cornbread

Serves: 2 | Prep & Cook time: 30 Min

- 100g cornmeal
- 100g plain flour
- 1 tablespoon granulated sugar
- 1 teaspoon baking powder
- 1/2 teaspoon salt
- 150ml milk
- 1 large egg
- 2 tablespoons unsalted butter, melted
- Cooking spray or oil for greasing.

DIRECTIONS:

1. In a mixing bowl, whisk together the cornmeal, plain flour, granulated sugar, baking powder, and salt.
2. In a separate bowl, whisk together the milk, egg, and melted butter.
3. Pour the wet ingredients into the dry ingredients and mix until just combined. Do not overmix.
4. Lightly grease a small baking dish or cake pan that fits in Zone 1 with cooking spray or a small amount of oil.
5. Pour the batter into the greased dish, spreading it evenly.
6. Place the baking dish in Zone 1 of the Ninja Dual Zone Air Fryer.
7. Select Zone 1, choose the BAKE program, and set the temperature to 180°C. Set the time to 15-20 minutes. Press the START/STOP button to begin cooking.
8. Check the cornbread after 15 minutes by inserting a toothpick into the center. If it comes out clean, it is done. If not, continue cooking for an additional 3-5 minutes.
9. Once cooked, carefully remove the cornbread from the air fryer and let it cool in the dish for a few minutes.
10. Cut the **cornbread** into squares or wedges and serve warm.

Turkey Ham Muffins

Serves: 4 | Prep & Cook time: 25 Min

- 2 large eggs
- 120ml milk
- 100g grated cheddar cheese
- 100g turkey ham, diced
- 200g self-raising flour
- 1 teaspoon baking powder
- 1/2 teaspoon salt
- 60ml vegetable oil
- 2 spring onions, finely chopped
- Optional: additional grated cheese for topping.

DIRECTIONS:

1. In a mixing bowl, combine the self-raising flour, baking powder, and salt. Mix well.
2. In a separate bowl, whisk together the milk, eggs, and vegetable oil.
3. Pour the wet ingredients into the dry ingredients and mix until just combined.
4. Fold in the grated cheddar cheese, diced turkey ham, and chopped spring onions.
5. Grease the muffin molds with a small amount of oil or cooking spray.
6. Spoon the muffin batter into the molds, filling each about three-quarters full.
7. Place the muffin molds in Zone 1 of the Ninja Dual Zone Air Fryer.
8. Select Zone 1, choose the BAKE program, and set the temperature to 180°C. Set the time to 12-15 minutes.
9. Press the START/STOP button to begin cooking.
10. Check the muffins after 12 minutes to see if they are golden brown and cooked through. If not, cook for an additional 1-3 minutes.
11. Once cooked, carefully remove the muffins from the air fryer and let them cool in the molds for a few minutes.
12. After cooling slightly, remove the **muffins** from the molds and let them cool on a wire rack.
13. If desired, sprinkle additional grated cheese on top of the muffins while they are still warm.

Sausage Egg Cup

Serves: 6 | Prep & Cook time: 25 Min

- 6 large eggs
- 100g cheddar cheese, grated
- 6 sausage links (pork or chicken)
- 1/2 red bell pepper, diced
- 1/2 onion, diced
- 1/2 green bell pepper, diced
- Salt and pepper to taste
- Fresh parsley, chopped (for garnish)

DIRECTIONS:

1. In a skillet, cook the sausage links over medium heat until browned and fully cooked. Remove from the skillet and let them cool slightly.
2. Cut the cooked sausages into small pieces.
3. In a bowl, whisk the eggs until well beaten. Season with salt and pepper.
4. Grease or line six individual ramekins or silicone cupcake liners.
5. Divide the diced bell peppers, onion, cooked sausage pieces, and grated cheddar cheese among the ramekins.
6. Pour the beaten eggs evenly into each ramekin, covering the ingredients.
7. Place 3 ramekins in each zone of the air fryer.
8. Select Zone 1, choose the BAKE program, and set the temperature to 180°C. Set the time to 15 minutes. Select MATCH. Press START/STOP to begin cooking.
9. When the cooking time is complete, remove the ramekins from the Air Fryer using oven mitts or tongs, as they will be hot.
10. Let the Sausage Egg Cups cool for a minute or two, then sprinkle with fresh parsley for garnish.
11. Serve the **Sausage Egg Cups** hot as a delicious breakfast or brunch option.

Pizza Eggs

Serves: 2-4 | Prep & Cook time: 20 Min

- 4 large eggs
- 4 tablespoons tomato sauce
- 4 tablespoons sliced black olives
- 4 tablespoons grated mozzarella cheese
- 4 tablespoons chopped bell peppers
- 4 tablespoons sliced mushrooms
- 4 tablespoons sliced pepperoni or cooked bacon
- Salt and pepper, to taste
- Fresh basil leaves, for garnish (optional)

DIRECTIONS:

1. Lightly grease the crisper plate in Zone 1 of the Air Fryer.
2. Crack one egg into each quadrant of the crisper plate, ensuring they are evenly spaced.
3. Spoon 1 tablespoon of tomato sauce over each egg.
4. Sprinkle 1 tablespoon of grated mozzarella cheese over each egg.
5. Top each egg with 1 tablespoon each of chopped bell peppers, sliced black olives, sliced mushrooms, and sliced pepperoni or cooked bacon.
6. Season with salt and pepper to taste.
7. Close the Air Fryer and select the BAKE program for Zone 1. Set the temperature to 180°C and the cooking time to 10 minutes.
8. Cook until the eggs are set and the cheese is melted and bubbly.
9. Carefully remove the crisper plate from the Air Fryer using oven mitts or tongs.
10. Garnish with fresh basil leaves, if desired.
11. Serve the **Pizza Eggs** hot as a delicious and savory breakfast or brunch option.

Bacon, Broccoli & Cheese Bread Pudding

Serves: 3 | Prep & Cook time: 25 Min

- 4 large eggs
- 240ml milk
- 4 slices of bread, preferably stale or day-old
- 4 slices of bacon, cooked and crumbled
- 100g broccoli florets, blanched and chopped
- 100g grated cheddar cheese
- 1/2 teaspoon Dijon mustard
- 1/2 teaspoon dried thyme
- Salt and pepper, to taste.

DIRECTIONS:

1. Lightly grease a baking dish that fits in Zone 1 of the Air Fryer.
2. Cut the bread slices into cubes and spread them evenly in the greased baking dish.
3. Sprinkle the crumbled bacon, chopped broccoli florets, and grated cheddar cheese over the bread cubes.
4. In a separate bowl, whisk together the eggs, milk, Dijon mustard, dried thyme, salt, and pepper.
5. Pour the egg mixture over the bread mixture in the baking dish, ensuring everything is evenly coated.
6. Place the baking dish in Zone 1 of the Air Fryer.
7. Close the Air Fryer and select the Bake program for Zone 1. Set the temperature to 180°C and the cooking time to 25 minutes.
8. Cook until the bread pudding is golden brown and set in the center.
9. Carefully remove the baking dish from the Air Fryer using oven mitts or tongs.
10. Allow the bread pudding to cool for a few minutes before serving.
11. Serve the **Bacon, Broccoli & Cheese Bread Pudding** warm as a delicious and satisfying meal.

Cheese & Ham Toasted Sandwiches

Serves: 2 | Prep & Cook time: 20 Min

- 2 teaspoons olive oil
- 1 garlic clove, bashed
- 75g cavolo nero, tough stalks removed
- 4 thick slices sourdough
- 2 teaspoons unsalted butter, softened
- 1 tablespoon dijon mustard
- 150g sliced smoked ham
- 100g brie, sliced
- 1 tablespoon red onion or tomato chutney

DIRECTIONS:

1. Heat the oil in a frying pan over a medium heat. Roughly chop the cavolo nero and add to the pan with the garlic, 1 tablespoon water and a pinch of salt and fry for about 3-4 minutes, stirring regularly until wilted. Discard the garlic and set aside.
2. To assemble the sandwiches, spread one side of each slice of sourdough with butter and place butter-side down on chopping board. Next, spread two of the slices with mustard, then layer them up with ham, cavolo nero and brie.
3. Spread the chutney on the remaining slices of sourdough, then sit on top of the sandwiches (with the butter on the outside). Press down firmly to compact the filling.
4. Place 1 sandwich in zone 1 drawer. Place the other sandwich in zone 2 drawer, then insert drawer in unit.
5. Select zone 1, select AIR FRY and set temperature to 200°C and set time to 6 minutes. Select MATCH. Press the START/STOP.
6. When zone 1 and zone 2 time reaches 3 minutes, remove drawer from unit and carefully turn the sandwiches using silicone-tipped tongs. Reinsert drawers to continue cooking.
7. When cooking is complete, remove the sandwiches from the drawers and cool for a couple of minutes, before cutting in half and serving

Bunless Turkey Burgers

Serves: 4 | Prep & Cook time: 35 Min

- 500g ground turkey
- 1/2 onion, finely chopped
- 1/2 red bell pepper, finely chopped
- 2 cloves garlic, minced
- 1 teaspoon dried thyme
- 1 teaspoon dried sage
- 1/2 teaspoon paprika
- Salt and pepper to taste
- 4 large eggs
- 4 slices cheddar cheese
- Fresh lettuce leaves
- Sliced tomatoes
- Sliced avocado
- Ketchup or your preferred sauce (optional)
- Olive oil, for spraying

DIRECTIONS:

1. In a mixing bowl, combine the ground turkey, chopped onion, chopped red bell pepper, minced garlic, dried thyme, dried sage, paprika, salt, and pepper. Mix until well combined.
2. Divide the turkey mixture into four equal portions and shape them into patties.
3. Spray the patties with olive oil to help them brown and prevent sticking.
4. Place the turkey patties in Zone 1 of the Air Fryer.
5. Select Zone 1, choose the AIR FRY program, and set the temperature to 200°C. Set the time to 20 minutes. Press START/STOP to begin cooking.
6. While the turkey burgers are cooking, prepare the eggs. In Zone 2 of the Air Fryer, crack the eggs and season with salt and pepper.
7. Select Zone 2, choose the AIR FRY program, and set the temperature to 180°C. Set the time to 5 minutes. Press START/STOP to begin cooking the eggs.
8. When the cooking time for the turkey burgers is almost finished, place a slice of cheddar cheese on each patty and let it melt slightly.
9. Remove the turkey burgers and eggs from the Air Fryer.
10. Assemble the bunless turkey burgers by placing each patty on a lettuce leaf.
11. Top with a fried egg, sliced tomatoes, sliced avocado, and any other desired toppings.
12. Serve the **bunless breakfast turkey burgers** with ketchup or your preferred sauce, if desired.

Cinnamon-Raisin Bagels

Serves: 4 | Prep & Cook time: 35 Min

- 300g bread flour
- 180ml warm water
- 1 1/2 teaspoons instant yeast
- 1 tablespoon granulated sugar
- 1/2 teaspoon ground cinnamon
- 100g raisins
- 1 tablespoon honey
- 1 tablespoon boiling water
- 1/2 teaspoon salt
- 1 egg, beaten (for egg wash)

DIRECTIONS:

1. In a large mixing bowl, combine the bread flour, instant yeast, granulated sugar, salt, ground cinnamon, and raisins.
2. Make a well in the center and pour in the warm water. Mix with a wooden spoon or your hands until a dough forms.
3. Transfer the dough to a lightly floured surface and knead for about 5-7 minutes until smooth and elastic.
4. Divide the dough into 4 equal portions and shape each portion into a ball. Flatten the balls slightly to form bagel shapes with a hole in the center.
5. In a small bowl, dissolve the honey in boiling water. Brush the bagels with the honey-water mixture using a pastry brush.
6. Place the bagels on a parchment-lined tray and transfer them to Zone 1 of the Air Fryer.
7. Select Zone 1, choose the BAKE program, and set the temperature to 200°C. Set the time to 15 minutes.
8. Press START/STOP to begin cooking.
9. After 8 minutes of cooking, remove the tray from the Air Fryer and brush the bagels with beaten egg wash.
10. Return the tray to the Air Fryer and continue cooking for the remaining 7 minutes.
11. When the cooking time is complete, remove the bagels from the Air Fryer and let them cool on a wire rack.
12. Serve the **cinnamon-raisin bagels** and enjoy them plain or with your favorite spreads.

Cajun Breakfast Sausage

Serves: 8 | Prep & Cook time: 25 Min

- 500g ground pork
- 1 tablespoon Cajun seasoning
- 1/2 teaspoon garlic powder
- 1/2 teaspoon onion powder
- 1/2 teaspoon dried thyme
- 1/2 teaspoon dried oregano
- 1/2 teaspoon paprika
- 1/4 teaspoon cayenne pepper (adjust to taste)
- Salt and pepper to taste
- Olive oil, for spraying

DIRECTIONS:

1. In a mixing bowl, combine the ground pork, Cajun seasoning, garlic powder, onion powder, dried thyme, dried oregano, paprika, cayenne pepper, salt, and pepper. Mix well to ensure the seasonings are evenly distributed.
2. Divide the mixture into 8 equal portions and shape each portion into a sausage patty.
3. Evenly dividing them between the two zone. Select Zone 1, choose the AIR FRY program, and set the temperature to 200°C. Set the time to 15 minutes.
4. Select MATCH to duplicate settings across both zones. Press START/STOP to begin cooking.
5. After 7 minutes of cooking, flip the sausage patties using tongs to ensure even browning.
6. Spray the patties with a little olive oil to help them crisp up.
7. Return the trays to the Air Fryer and continue cooking for the remaining 8 minutes.
8. When the cooking time is complete, remove the sausage patties from the Air Fryer and let them cool for a few minutes.
9. Serve the **Cajun breakfast sausage** patties hot with your preferred breakfast accompaniments.

English Muffins

Serves: 4 | Prep & Cook time: 35 Min

- 450g strong white bread flour
- 1 teaspoon salt
- 2 teaspoons caster sugar
- 2 teaspoons instant yeast
- 225ml warm milk
- 1 tablespoon melted butter
- Semolina or cornmeal, for dusting.

DIRECTIONS:

1. In a large mixing bowl, combine the bread flour, salt, caster sugar, and instant yeast.
2. Make a well in the center of the dry ingredients and pour in the warm milk and melted butter.
3. Mix the ingredients together using a wooden spoon until a soft dough forms.
4. Turn the dough out onto a lightly floured surface and knead for about 5 minutes until smooth and elastic.
5. Divide the dough into 4 equal portions and shape each portion into a round ball.
6. Place the dough balls onto a baking tray lined with parchment paper and lightly dusted with semolina or cornmeal.
7. Place the baking tray with the dough balls into Zone 1 of the Air Fryer.
8. Select Zone 1, choose the BAKE and set the temperature to 180°C. Set the time to 15 minutes. Press START/STOP to begin cooking.
9. Once they are golden brown and cooked through, remove the English muffins from the Air Fryer and allow them to cool on a wire rack.
10. To serve, split the **English muffins** in half and toast them. They can be enjoyed with butter, jam, or your favorite toppings.

Spinach Omelet

Serves: 2 | Prep & Cook time: 20 Min

- 4 large eggs
- 100g fresh spinach leaves
- 50g grated cheddar cheese
- 1 small onion, diced
- 1 tablespoon butter
- Salt and pepper to taste
- Fresh parsley, chopped (for garnish)

DIRECTIONS:

1. In a bowl, beat the eggs and season with salt and pepper.
2. Place the diced onion in Zone 1 of the Air Fryer and select AIR FRY. Set the temperature to 180°C. Cook for about 3-5 minutes until the onion becomes translucent.
3. Add the fresh spinach leaves to Zone 1 of the Air Fryer with the cooked onions. Cook for an additional 2 minutes until the spinach wilts.
4. Transfer the cooked onions and spinach to a separate bowl.
5. In Zone 2 of the Air Fryer, melt the butter using AIR FRY program. Set the temperature to 180°C. Time: 1 minute. Press START/STOP to begin cooking.
6. Pour the beaten eggs into Zone 2 with the melted butter and cook for 2 minutes, or until the edges start to set.
7. Sprinkle the cooked onions, spinach, and grated cheddar cheese evenly over one half of the omelet in Zone 2.
8. Close the Air Fryer and continue cooking for an additional 3-4 minutes, or until the omelet is cooked through and the cheese has melted.
9. Carefully remove the omelet from the Air Fryer and fold it in half.
10. Garnish with fresh chopped parsley.
11. Serve the **Spinach Omelet** warm as a delicious breakfast or brunch option.

Asparagus & Bell Pepper Strata

Serves: 4 | Prep & Cook time: 40 Min

- 6 slices of bread, cubed
- 1 bunch of asparagus, trimmed and cut into bite-sized pieces
- 1 red bell pepper, diced
- 1 yellow bell pepper, diced
- 110g grated cheddar cheese
- 4 large eggs
- 350 ml milk
- 1 teaspoon Dijon mustard
- 1/2 teaspoon dried thyme
- Salt and pepper to taste
- Olive oil, for greasing

DIRECTIONS:

1. Grease the cooking tray in Zone 1 with a little olive oil.
2. In a large bowl, combine the bread cubes, asparagus, bell peppers, and grated cheddar cheese. Mix well.
3. In a separate bowl, whisk together the eggs, milk, Dijon mustard, dried thyme, salt, and pepper.
4. Pour the egg mixture over the bread mixture and stir until all the ingredients are evenly coated.
5. Transfer the mixture to the greased tray in Zone 1 of the Air Fryer.
6. Select Zone 1, choose the BAKE program, and set the temperature to 180°C. Set the time to 25 minutes.
7. Press START/STOP to begin cooking.
8. When the cooking time is complete, carefully remove the tray from the Air Fryer using oven mitts.
9. Allow the strata to cool for a few minutes before serving.
10. Serve the **Asparagus and Bell Pepper Strata** as a delicious and satisfying breakfast or brunch option.

Pancake Cake

Serves: 4 | Prep & Cook time: 35 Min

- 200g self-raising flour
- 2 tablespoons caster sugar
- 1 teaspoon baking powder
- 1/4 teaspoon salt
- 2 large eggs
- 300ml milk
- 1 teaspoon vanilla extract
- Butter or oil, for greasing
- Desired toppings (e.g., fresh berries, sliced bananas, maple syrup, yogurt)

DIRECTIONS:

1. In a mixing bowl, combine the self-raising flour, caster sugar, baking powder, and salt.
2. In a separate bowl, whisk together the eggs, milk, and vanilla extract until well combined.
3. Gradually pour the wet ingredients into the dry ingredients while whisking continuously, until a smooth batter is formed.
4. Preheat both zones of the Ninja Dual Zone Air Fryer at 180°C.
5. Lightly grease both zones with butter or oil.
6. Divide the pancake batter evenly into 2 halves, pour into 2 zones, spreading it evenly.
7. Close the Air Fryer and select the BAKE program for Zone 1. Set the temperature to 180°C and the cooking time to 10 minutes. Select MATCH. Press START/STOP to begin cooking.
8. While the pancakes are cooking, prepare your desired toppings.
9. Once the pancakes are cooked, carefully remove them from the Air Fryer using a spatula or tongs.
10. Layer the pancakes on a serving plate, adding your desired toppings between each layer.
11. Serve the **Pancake Cake** warm with additional toppings, such as fresh berries, sliced bananas, maple syrup, or yogurt.

Egg Tarts

Serves: 2 | Prep & Cook time: 35 Min

- 200g ready-made shortcrust pastry
- 2 large eggs
- 100ml double cream
- 30g caster sugar
- 1/2 teaspoon vanilla extract
- Pinch of salt
- Icing sugar (for dusting)

DIRECTIONS:

1. Roll out the shortcrust pastry on a lightly floured surface until it is approximately 3-4mm thick.
2. Cut out two circles of pastry that are slightly larger than your tart molds.
3. Line the tart molds with the pastry circles, gently pressing them into the bottom and sides. Trim any excess pastry.
4. In a mixing bowl, whisk together the eggs, double cream, caster sugar, vanilla extract, and salt until well combined.
5. Pour the egg mixture evenly into the prepared tart molds.
6. Place the filled tart molds in Zone 1 of the Air Fryer and select BAKE. Set the temperature to 180°C
7. Bake for 18-20 minutes, or until the egg tarts are set and the pastry is golden brown.
8. Once cooked, carefully remove the tart molds from the Air Fryer and let them cool for a few minutes.
9. Dust the egg tarts with icing sugar.
10. Serve the **Egg Tarts** warm or chilled as a delightful sweet treat.

Red Pepper & Feta Frittata

Serves: 4 | Prep & Cook time: 28 Min

- 6 large eggs
- 100ml milk
- 1 red bell pepper, diced
- 100g feta cheese, crumbled
- 1 small red onion, finely chopped
- Handful of fresh parsley, chopped
- Salt and pepper, to taste
- Olive oil, for greasing

DIRECTIONS:

1. In a large mixing bowl, whisk together the eggs and milk until well combined.
2. Add the diced red bell pepper, crumbled feta cheese, chopped red onion, and fresh parsley to the egg mixture. Season with salt and pepper to taste. Stir until all ingredients are evenly distributed.
3. Lightly grease a baking dish that fits into Zone 1 of the Air Fryer with olive oil.
4. Pour the egg mixture into the greased baking dish, spreading it out evenly.
5. Place the baking dish in Zone 1 of the Air Fryer and select BAKE. Set the temperature to 180°C.
6. Bake for 15-18 minutes, or until the frittata is set and slightly golden on top.
7. Once cooked, carefully remove the baking dish from the Air Fryer and let it cool for a few minutes.
8. Cut the **frittata** into wedges and serve warm as a delicious breakfast or brunch option.

Fried Chicken Wings with Waffles

Serves: 4 | Prep & Cook time: 40 Min

For the Chicken Wings:

- 800g chicken wings
- 150g all-purpose flour
- 1 teaspoon paprika
- 1 teaspoon garlic powder
- 1 teaspoon onion powder
- 1/2 teaspoon salt
- 1/4 teaspoon black pepper
- Vegetable oil, for spraying

For the Waffles:

- 200g plain flour
- 2 tablespoons granulated sugar
- 1 tablespoon baking powder
- 1/2 teaspoon salt
- 300ml milk
- 2 large eggs
- 60g unsalted butter, melted
- Vegetable oil, for spraying

For Serving:

- Maple syrup
- Butter

DIRECTIONS

1. In a mixing bowl, combine the flour, paprika, garlic powder, onion powder, salt, and black pepper for the chicken wings coating.
2. Dip each chicken wing into the flour mixture, coating it evenly. Shake off any excess flour.
3. Place the coated chicken wings in Zone 1 of the Air Fryer.
4. Select Zone 1, choose the AIR FRY program, and set the temperature to 200°C. Set the time to 25 minutes.
5. Press START/STOP to begin cooking.
6. While the chicken wings are cooking, prepare the waffle batter. In a separate bowl, whisk together the flour, sugar, baking powder, and salt for the waffles.
7. In another bowl, whisk together the milk, eggs, and melted butter. Pour the wet ingredients into the dry ingredients and mix until just combined.
8. Lightly grease the waffle plates in Zone 2 of the Air Fryer with cooking spray or melted butter.
9. Pour the waffle batter onto the greased plates, spreading it out evenly.
10. Close the Air Fryer and select the BAKE program for Zone 2. Set the temperature to 180°C and the cooking time to 10-12 minutes.
11. Cook until the waffles are golden brown and cooked through.
12. Remove the cooked chicken wings and waffles from the Air Fryer.
13. Serve the crispy fried chicken wings with the freshly made waffles.
14. Top with a pat of butter and drizzle with maple syrup.
15. Enjoy the delicious combination of **crispy chicken wings and fluffy waffles!**

Cinnamon Rolls

Serves: 12 rolls | Prep & Cook time: 42 Min

For the dough:

- 1 large egg
- 250ml warm milk
- 500g strong white bread flour
- 7g instant yeast
- 50g granulated sugar
- 1 teaspoon salt
- 50g unsalted butter, melted.

For the filling:

- 75g unsalted butter, softened
- 150g light brown sugar
- 2 tablespoons ground cinnamon.

For the glaze:

- 200g icing sugar
- 2-3 tablespoons milk
- 1 teaspoon vanilla extract.

DIRECTIONS

1. In a large mixing bowl, combine the bread flour, instant yeast, granulated sugar, and salt.
2. Make a well in the center of the dry ingredients and pour in the warm milk, melted butter, and egg.
3. Mix the ingredients together until a dough forms.
4. Turn the dough out onto a floured surface and knead for about 5 minutes until smooth and elastic.
5. Place the dough back in the bowl, cover with a clean kitchen towel, and let it rest for 10 minutes.
6. Roll out the dough into a rectangle approximately 30cm x 40cm in size.
7. Spread the softened butter evenly over the dough.
8. In a small bowl, mix together the light brown sugar and ground cinnamon. Sprinkle this mixture over the buttered dough, covering it completely.
9. Starting from one long side, tightly roll the dough into a log shape.
10. Cut the log into 12 equal-sized rolls. Place 6 rolls in each zone of the air fryer.
11. Select Zone 1, choose the BAKE program, and set the temperature to 180°C. Set the time to 12 minutes. Select MATCH. Press START/STOP to begin cooking.
12. While the rolls are cooking, prepare the glaze by whisking together the icing sugar, milk, and vanilla extract until smooth.
13. After the cooking time is complete, remove drawers from the Air Fryer and let the rolls cool for a few minutes.
14. Drizzle the glaze over the warm cinnamon rolls.
15. Serve the **Cinnamon Rolls** while still warm and enjoy their sweet, spiced goodness.

Air Fried Broccoli

Serves: 1 | Prep & Cook time: 15 Min

- 200g broccoli florets
- 1 tablespoon olive oil
- 1/2 teaspoon garlic powder
- 1/2 teaspoon paprika
- Salt and pepper to taste
- Lemon wedges, for serving (optional)

DIRECTIONS:

1. In a bowl, toss the broccoli florets with olive oil, garlic powder, paprika, salt, and pepper. Ensure the florets are evenly coated.
2. Place the seasoned broccoli florets in Zone 1 of the air fryer basket. Select the AIR FRY program. Set the temperature to 180°C. Set the cooking time to 12 minutes. Press START/STOP to begin cooking.
3. While the broccoli is cooking, you can prepare any additional dishes or sides.
4. Once the cooking time is complete, remove the air fryer basket from Zone 1 and transfer the air-fried broccoli to a serving plate.
5. Serve the **air-fried broccoli** hot, optionally with a squeeze of fresh lemon juice for added flavor.

Chapter 2: Everyday Favourites & Sides

Scalloped Veggie Mix

Serves: 4 | Prep & Cook time: 35 Min

- 500g mixed vegetables (such as carrots, broccoli, cauliflower)
- 1 tablespoon butter
- 1 tablespoon all-purpose flour
- 250ml milk
- 100g grated cheese (such as cheddar or Gruyere)
- 1/2 teaspoon garlic powder
- Salt and pepper to taste
- Fresh parsley, chopped (for garnish)

DIRECTIONS:

1. In a pot of boiling water, cook the mixed vegetables until they are slightly tender. Drain and set aside.
2. In a separate saucepan, melt the butter over medium heat. Stir in the flour and cook for 1-2 minutes until it forms a paste.
3. Gradually whisk in the milk until the mixture becomes smooth and thickens. Cook for an additional 2-3 minutes, stirring constantly.
4. Remove the saucepan from the heat and stir in the grated cheese until it melts and forms a creamy sauce. Season with garlic powder, salt, and pepper.
5. In Zone 1 of the air fryer basket, layer half of the cooked vegetables. Pour half of the cheese sauce over the vegetables.
6. Repeat the layering process with the remaining vegetables and cheese sauce in Zone 2.
7. Select zone 1, select BAKE and set temperature to 180°C and set time to 25 minutes. Select MATCH to duplicate settings across both zones. Press the START/STOP button to begin cooking.
8. Once the cooking time is complete, remove the air fryer basket and let it cool for a few minutes.
9. Garnish with fresh chopped parsley and serve the **Scalloped Veggie Mix** hot.

Indian-Style Sweet Potato Fries

Serves: 20 fries | Prep & Cook time: 20 Min

- 2 large sweet potatoes
- 2 tablespoons olive oil
- 1 teaspoon ground cumin
- 1 teaspoon ground coriander
- 1/2 teaspoon ground turmeric
- 1/2 teaspoon paprika
- 1/2 teaspoon salt
- Freshly ground black pepper to taste
- Chopped fresh coriander (cilantro), for garnish (optional)
- Lime wedges, for serving

DIRECTIONS:

1. Wash and peel the sweet potatoes. Cut them into thin, even-sized fries.
2. In a bowl, combine the olive oil, ground cumin, ground coriander, ground turmeric, paprika, salt, and black pepper. Mix well to form a spice mixture.
3. Place the sweet potato fries in a large bowl and drizzle the spice mixture over them. Toss until the fries are evenly coated with the spices.
4. Divide the sweet potato fries evenly between Zones 1 and 2 of the air fryer basket. Spread them out in a single layer for even cooking.
5. Select zone 1, select AIR FRY and set temperature to 200°C and set time to 15 minutes. Select MATCH to duplicate settings across both zones. Press the START/STOP button to begin cooking.
6. After 10 minutes, carefully remove the basket and shake it to ensure even cooking. Return the basket to the air fryer and continue cooking for the remaining 5 minutes or until the fries are crispy and golden brown.
7. Once cooked, remove the **Indian-Style Sweet Potato Fries** from the Air Fryer and transfer them to a serving dish.
8. Garnish with chopped fresh coriander (cilantro), if desired, and serve hot with lime wedges on the side for added zest.

Bacon Pinwheels

Serves: 8 pinwheels | Prep & Cook time: 25 Min

- 1 sheet ready-made puff pastry
- 8 slices streaky bacon
- 100 grams grated Cheddar cheese
- 1 tablespoon Dijon mustard
- Freshly ground black pepper, to taste
- Chopped fresh parsley, for garnish (optional)

DIRECTIONS:

1. Lay out the sheet of puff pastry on a clean surface. Spread the Dijon mustard evenly over the puff pastry.
2. Sprinkle the grated Cheddar cheese over the mustard, making sure to cover the entire surface of the puff pastry.
3. Season with freshly ground black pepper to taste.
4. Starting from one end, tightly roll up the puff pastry into a log shape.
5. Cut the rolled puff pastry log into 8 equal-sized slices.
6. Take a slice of streaky bacon and wrap it around one of the puff pastry slices, ensuring the bacon covers the entire slice.
7. Repeat the process for the remaining puff pastry slices and bacon.
8. Place the bacon-wrapped puff pastry pinwheels in both zone1 of the air fryer basket, making sure they are spaced apart.
9. Select zone 1, select AIR FRY and set temperature to 200°C and set time to 15 minutes. Select MATCH to duplicate settings across both zones. Press the START/STOP button to begin cooking.
10. After 10 minutes, carefully remove the basket and flip the bacon pinwheels to ensure even cooking. Return the basket to the air fryer and continue cooking for the remaining 5 minutes or until the bacon is crispy and the puff pastry is golden brown.
11. Once cooked, remove the **Bacon Pinwheels** from the Air Fryer and transfer them to a serving dish.
12. Garnish with chopped fresh parsley, if desired, serve hot as a delicious appetizer or snack.

Glazed Sweet Potato Bites

Serves: 4 | Prep & Cook time: 35 Min

- 2 medium-sized sweet potatoes
- 2 tablespoons olive oil
- 2 tablespoons maple syrup
- 1 teaspoon ground cinnamon
- 1/2 teaspoon ground nutmeg
- 1/2 teaspoon salt
- 1/4 teaspoon black pepper
- Fresh parsley or coriander leaves for garnish (optional)

DIRECTIONS:

1. Peel the sweet potatoes and cut them into bite-sized cubes.
2. In a large bowl, combine the olive oil, maple syrup, ground cinnamon, ground nutmeg, salt, and black pepper. Mix well.
3. Add the sweet potato cubes to the bowl and toss them in the glaze mixture until they are evenly coated.
4. Preheat Zone 1 to 200°C.
5. Place the sweet potato cubes in Zone 1. Make sure they are arranged in a single layer for even cooking.
6. Select Zone 1, choose the AIR FRY function, set the temperature to 200°C. Time to 20 minutes. Flipping the sweet potato cubes halfway through the cooking time for even browning.
7. Once the sweet potato bites are crispy and caramelized, remove them from the air fryer and let them cool slightly.
8. Transfer the glazed sweet potato bites to a serving dish and garnish with fresh parsley or coriander leaves, if desired.
9. Serve the **Glazed Sweet Potato Bites** as a delicious side dish or appetizer.

Cheese-Walnut Stuffed Mushrooms

Serves: 4 | Prep & Cook time: 25 Min

- 8 large button mushrooms
- 50g grated cheddar cheese
- 25g breadcrumbs
- 25g chopped walnuts
- 1 tablespoon chopped fresh parsley
- 1 clove garlic, minced
- 1 tablespoon olive oil
- Salt and pepper to taste.

DIRECTIONS:

1. Remove the stems from the mushrooms and set them aside.
2. In a mixing bowl, combine the grated cheddar cheese, breadcrumbs, chopped walnuts, chopped parsley, minced garlic, olive oil, salt, and pepper. Mix well to form a stuffing mixture.
3. Fill each mushroom cap with a generous amount of the cheese-walnut stuffing mixture, pressing it gently to ensure it stays in place.
4. Finely chop the reserved mushroom stems and distribute them evenly over the stuffed mushrooms.
5. Place the stuffed mushrooms in Zone 1 of the Ninja Dual Zone air fryer. Make sure they are arranged in a single layer.
6. Select Zone 1, choose the AIR FRY function, set the temperature to 180°C. Time to 12 minutes, until the mushrooms are tender and the cheese is melted and lightly golden.
7. Once cooked, carefully remove the stuffed mushrooms from the air fryer and let them cool for a few minutes before serving.
8. Serve the **Cheese-Walnut Stuffed Mushrooms** as a delicious appetizer or side dish.

Gold Artichoke Hearts

Serves: 4 | Prep & Cook time: 25 Min

- 2 cans of artichoke hearts (400g total), drained and rinsed
- 2 tablespoons olive oil
- 1 teaspoon garlic powder
- 1 teaspoon dried thyme
- 1/2 teaspoon salt
- 1/4 teaspoon black pepper
- Lemon wedges, for serving.

DIRECTIONS:

1. In a bowl, combine the olive oil, garlic powder, dried thyme, salt, and black pepper.
2. Add the drained and rinsed artichoke hearts to the bowl and toss to coat them evenly with the seasoned oil mixture.
3. Lightly grease the air fryer basket in Zone 1. Place the seasoned artichoke hearts in the greased air fryer basket.
4. Select Zone 1, choose the AIR FRY function, set the temperature to 200°C, cooking time to 15 minutes. Press the START/STOP.
5. Halfway through the cooking time, gently shake the air fryer basket to ensure even cooking.
6. After the cooking time is complete, carefully remove the Gold Artichoke Hearts from the air fryer using tongs or a spatula.
7. Serve the crispy **Gold Artichoke Hearts** as a delightful appetizer or side dish. Squeeze fresh lemon juice over them for added flavor, if desired.

Fried Brussels Sprouts

Serves: 4 | Prep & Cook time: 25 Min

- 500g Brussels sprouts, trimmed and halved
- 2 tablespoons olive oil
- 1 teaspoon garlic powder
- 1/2 teaspoon paprika
- 1/2 teaspoon salt
- 1/4 teaspoon black pepper
- Lemon wedges, for serving.

DIRECTIONS:

1. In a large bowl, toss the Brussels sprouts with olive oil, garlic powder, paprika, salt, and black pepper until well coated.
2. Lightly grease the air fryer basket in Zone 1 of the Ninja Dual Zone Air Fryer.
3. Place the seasoned Brussels sprouts in the greased air fryer basket. (if overcrowded, put the rest to zone 2 and cook on both zones)
4. Select Zone 1, choose the AIR FRY function, set the temperature to 200°C, cooking time to 15 minutes. Press the START/STOP.
5. Halfway through the cooking time, gently shake the air fryer basket to ensure even cooking.
6. After the cooking time is complete, carefully remove the Fried Brussels Sprouts from the air fryer using tongs or a spatula.
7. Serve the crispy **Fried Brussels Sprouts** as a delicious side dish. Squeeze fresh lemon juice over them for added brightness, if desired.

Potato with Creamy Cheese

Serves: 2 | Prep & Cook time: 40 Min

- 2 large potatoes, washed and thinly sliced
- 100g grated cheddar cheese
- 60ml sour cream
- 30g butter, melted
- 2 tablespoons chopped fresh chives
- Salt and pepper to taste.

DIRECTIONS:

1. In a bowl, combine the grated cheddar cheese, sour cream, melted butter, chopped fresh chives, salt, and pepper. Mix well to create a creamy cheese mixture.
2. Place the thinly sliced potatoes in a separate bowl and season them with salt and pepper.
3. Take one potato slice and spread a layer of the creamy cheese mixture on top. Place another potato slice on top and repeat the process until you have a stack of potato slices with the cheese mixture in between.
4. Repeat the process for the remaining potato slices and cheese mixture, creating multiple potato stacks.
5. Lightly grease the air fryer basket in Zone 1 of Air Fryer.
6. Place the potato stacks in a single layer in the greased air fryer basket.
7. Select Zone 1, choose the AIR FRY function, and set the temperature to 180°C, cooking time to 30 minutes. Press the START/STOP.
8. After the cooking time is complete, carefully remove the Potato with Creamy Cheese stacks from the air fryer using tongs or a spatula.
9. Serve the **Potato with Creamy Cheese** as a delightful side dish or as a main course. The potatoes will be crispy on the outside and tender on the inside, complemented by the creamy and cheesy filling.

Balsamic Brussels Sprouts

Serves: 4 | Prep & Cook time: 25 Min

- 500g Brussels sprouts, trimmed and halved
- 2 tablespoons olive oil
- 2 tablespoons balsamic vinegar
- 1 tablespoon honey
- 2 cloves garlic, minced
- Salt and pepper to taste.

DIRECTIONS:

1. In a bowl, whisk together the olive oil, balsamic vinegar, honey, minced garlic, salt, and pepper to create a marinade.
2. Place the Brussels sprouts in a separate bowl and pour the marinade over them. Toss well to ensure the Brussels sprouts are evenly coated.
3. Lightly grease the air fryer basket in Zone 1.
4. Place the Brussels sprouts in a single layer in the greased air fryer basket. (if overcrowded, put the rest to zone 2 and cook on both zones)
5. Select Zone 1, choose the AIR FRY, set the temperature to 200°C, cooking time to 15 minutes. Press the START/STOP.
6. Halfway through the cooking time, gently shake the air fryer basket to ensure even cooking.
7. After the cooking time is complete, carefully remove the Balsamic Brussels Sprouts from the air fryer using tongs or a spatula.
8. Serve the **Balsamic Brussels Sprouts** as a delicious side dish. They will have a crispy exterior and a tender interior with a tangy and slightly sweet flavor from the balsamic marinade.

Garlic Herb Radishes

Serves: 4 | Prep & Cook time: 20 Min

- 1 bunch of radishes (about 400g), washed and trimmed
- 2 tablespoons olive oil
- 2 cloves garlic, minced
- 1 teaspoon dried herbs (such as thyme, rosemary, or parsley)
- Salt and pepper to taste.

DIRECTIONS:

1. Cut the radishes into halves or quarters, depending on their size. Ensure they are relatively uniform in size for even cooking
2. In a bowl, combine the olive oil, minced garlic, dried herbs, salt, and pepper. Mix well to make the garlic herb seasoning.
3. Toss the radishes in the garlic herb seasoning until they are evenly coated.
4. Lightly grease the cooking basket in Zone 1 of the Ninja Dual Zone Air Fryer with cooking spray or a small amount of oil.
5. Place the seasoned radishes in Zone 1's cooking basket in a single layer, ensuring they are not overcrowded. (if overcrowded, put the rest to zone 2 and cook on both zones)
6. Select Zone 1, choose the AIR FRY, and set the temperature to 200°C. Set the time to 12 minutes. Press the START/STOP.
7. Halfway through the cooking time, pause the air fryer and shake the basket to ensure even cooking. Then, continue cooking until the radishes are tender and golden brown.
8. Once the cooking time is complete, carefully remove the basket from the air fryer and let the Garlic Herb Radishes cool for a few minutes.
9. Serve the **Garlic Herb Radishes** as a flavorful side dish or incorporate them into salads and other dishes.

Crispy Garlic Sliced Aubergine

Serves: 4 | Prep & Cook time: 30 Min

- 2 medium-sized aubergines (eggplants)
- 4 cloves garlic, minced
- 2 tablespoons olive oil
- 2 tablespoons breadcrumbs
- 1 tablespoon grated Parmesan cheese
- 1 teaspoon dried oregano
- Salt and pepper to taste.

DIRECTIONS:

1. Wash the aubergines and cut them into 1/4-inch thick slices.
2. In a bowl, combine the minced garlic, olive oil, breadcrumbs, grated Parmesan cheese, dried oregano, salt, and pepper. Mix well to form a paste.
3. Brush both sides of the aubergine slices with the garlic paste mixture, ensuring they are well coated.
4. Lightly grease the air fryer basket in Zone 1 of the Ninja Dual Zone Air Fryer.
5. Place the coated aubergine slices in a single layer in the greased air fryer basket.
6. Select Zone 1, choose the AIR FRY function, temperature to 200°C, cooking time to 15 minutes. Press the START/STOP.
7. Halfway through the cooking time, flip the aubergine slices to ensure even browning.
8. After the cooking time is complete, carefully remove the crispy garlic sliced aubergine from the air fryer using tongs or a spatula.
9. Serve the **Crispy Garlic Sliced Aubergine** as a delicious side dish or as part of a meal. They are perfect for dipping in sauces or as a topping for salads.

Dijon Roast Cabbage

Serves: 4 | Prep & Cook time: 30 Min

- 1 small head of cabbage
- 2 tablespoons Dijon mustard
- 2 tablespoons olive oil
- 1 tablespoon honey
- 1 teaspoon garlic powder
- Salt and pepper to taste.

DIRECTIONS:

1. Cut the cabbage into wedges, leaving the core intact to hold the wedges together.
2. In a small bowl, whisk together the Dijon mustard, olive oil, honey, garlic powder, salt, and pepper until well combined.
3. Brush the Dijon mustard mixture over the cabbage wedges, making sure to coat all sides.
4. Place the cabbage wedges in Zone 1 of the Ninja Dual Zone Air Fryer in a single layer.
5. Select Zone 1, choose the ROAST function, and set the temperature to 200°C. Set the cooking time to 20 minutes. Press the START/STOP button to begin roasting.
6. After 10 minutes of cooking, open Zone 1 and flip the cabbage wedges using tongs for even browning.
7. Close Zone 1 and continue roasting for the remaining 10 minutes or until the cabbage is tender and lightly charred.
8. Once done, remove the **Dijon Roast Cabbage** from the air fryer and serve hot as a delicious side dish.

Crispy Chickpeas

Serves: 2 | Prep & Cook time: 20 Min

- 2 cans (400g each) chickpeas, drained and rinsed
- 2 tablespoons olive oil
- 1 teaspoon paprika
- 1/2 teaspoon cumin
- 1/2 teaspoon garlic powder
- 1/2 teaspoon onion powder
- 1/4 teaspoon cayenne pepper (adjust to taste)
- Salt to taste.

DIRECTIONS:

1. Preheat Zone 1 of the Ninja Dual Zone Air Fryer to 200°C.
2. In a bowl, toss the chickpeas with olive oil, paprika, cumin, garlic powder, onion powder, cayenne pepper, and salt until well coated.
3. Place the seasoned chickpeas in Zone 1 of the Ninja Dual Zone Air Fryer in a single layer.
4. Select Zone 1, choose the AIR FRY function, and set the temperature to 200°C. Set the cooking time to 15 minutes. Press the START/STOP.
5. After 7-8 minutes of cooking, open Zone 1 and shake the basket to ensure even cooking.
6. Close Zone 1 and continue air frying for the remaining 7-8 minutes or until the chickpeas are crispy and golden brown.
7. Once done, remove the crispy chickpeas from the air fryer and let them cool slightly before serving.
8. Serve the **crispy chickpeas** as a snack or use them as a topping for salads, soups, or roasted vegetables.

Fried Courgette Salad

Serves: 4 | Prep & Cook time: 20 Min

- 2 medium courgettes (zucchini), sliced into rounds
- 2 tablespoons plain flour
- 1/4 teaspoon salt
- 1/4 teaspoon black pepper
- 2 eggs, beaten
- 120g breadcrumbs
- 2 tablespoons grated Parmesan cheese
- 2 tablespoons olive oil
- Mixed salad greens
- Cherry tomatoes, halved
- Lemon wedges, for serving.

DIRECTIONS:

1. In a shallow bowl, combine the flour, salt, and black pepper. Place the beaten eggs in another bowl, and in a separate bowl, combine the breadcrumbs and grated Parmesan cheese.
2. Dip the courgette slices into the flour mixture, shaking off any excess. Then dip them into the beaten eggs, allowing any excess to drip off. Finally, coat the courgette slices in the breadcrumb mixture, pressing gently to adhere.
3. Place the coated courgette slices in Zone 1 of the Ninja Dual Zone Air Fryer in a single layer.
4. Select Zone 1, choose the AIR FRY function, and set the temperature to 200°C, cooking time to 10 minutes. Press the START/STOP.
5. After 5 minutes of cooking, open Zone 1 and flip the courgette slices to ensure even browning. Continue air frying for the remaining 5 minutes or until the courgettes are crispy and golden brown.
6. While the courgettes are frying, prepare the salad by combining mixed salad greens and cherry tomatoes in a serving bowl.
7. Once the courgettes are cooked, remove them from the air fryer and place them on a paper towel to absorb any excess oil.
8. Arrange the crispy courgette slices on top of the salad.
9. Serve the **fried courgette salad** with lemon wedges on the side for squeezing over the top.

Ricotta Potatoes

Serves: 4 | Prep & Cook time: 35 Min

- 4 medium-sized potatoes, washed and scrubbed
- 120g ricotta cheese
- 2 tablespoons grated Parmesan cheese
- 2 tablespoons chopped fresh parsley
- 1 clove garlic, minced
- 1/2 teaspoon salt
- 1/4 teaspoon black pepper
- 2 tablespoons olive oil.

DIRECTIONS:

1. Pierce the potatoes all over with a fork. Place them in Zone 1, choose the AIR FRY, temperature to 200°C and cook for 20 minutes or until the potatoes are tender.
2. Once the potatoes are cooked, remove them from the air fryer and let them cool slightly.
3. Cut each potato in half lengthwise. Using a spoon, scoop out the flesh of each potato, leaving a thin layer of potato intact along the skin.
4. In a bowl, combine the potato flesh, ricotta cheese, grated Parmesan cheese, chopped parsley, minced garlic, salt, and black pepper. Mix well until all ingredients are thoroughly combined.
5. Spoon the ricotta mixture back into the potato skins, filling them generously.
6. Place the stuffed potato halves in Zone 1. Select Zone 1, choose the AIR FRY, temperature to 200°C, cooking time to 5 minutes. Press the START/STOP.
7. After 2 minutes of cooking, open Zone 1 and drizzle the olive oil over the stuffed potato halves. Continue air frying for the remaining 3 minutes or until the tops are golden brown.
8. Once cooked, remove the **ricotta potatoes** from the air fryer and serve them hot.

Mushrooms with Goat Cheese

Serves: 4 | Prep & Cook time: 25 Min

- 8 large mushrooms, cleaned and stems removed
- 100g goat cheese, crumbled
- 2 tablespoons fresh parsley, chopped
- 2 tablespoons breadcrumbs
- 2 tablespoons grated Parmesan cheese
- 2 cloves of garlic, minced
- 2 tablespoons olive oil
- Salt and pepper, to taste.

DIRECTIONS:

1. In a bowl, combine the goat cheese, fresh parsley, breadcrumbs, grated Parmesan cheese, minced garlic, olive oil, salt, and pepper. Mix well until all the ingredients are evenly incorporated.
2. Stuff each mushroom cap with the prepared goat cheese mixture, filling it generously.
3. Place the stuffed mushrooms in Zone 1 of the air fryer basket.
4. Select Zone 1, choose the AIR FRY function, and set the temperature to 180°C. Set the cooking time to 12-15 minutes (until the mushrooms are tender and the cheese is melted and slightly golden). Press the START/STOP button to begin air frying.
5. Once cooked, remove the mushrooms from the air fryer and let them cool slightly.
6. Serve the **mushrooms with goat cheese** as a delicious appetizer or side dish.

Green Tomato Salad

Serves: 4 | Prep & Cook time: 25 Min

- 4 green tomatoes
- 1 small red onion
- 1/2 cucumber
- 25g fresh parsley, chopped
- 25g fresh mint leaves, chopped
- Juice of 1 lemon
- 2 tablespoons extra virgin olive oil
- Salt and pepper to taste.

DIRECTIONS:

1. Slice the green tomatoes into thin rounds. Finely chop the red onion. Cut the cucumber in half lengthwise, remove the seeds, and slice it into thin half-moons.
2. In a mixing bowl, combine the sliced green tomatoes, red onion, cucumber, chopped parsley, and chopped mint leaves.
3. In a separate small bowl, whisk together the lemon juice, extra virgin olive oil, salt, and pepper to make the dressing.
4. Pour the dressing over the salad mixture and toss well to combine, ensuring all the ingredients are coated evenly.
5. Place the salad plate in Zone 1. Set Zone 1 to the AIR FRY function, and adjust the temperature to 200°C. Cook for 10 minutes or until the tomatoes have softened slightly.
6. Once cooked, remove the plate from the air fryer.
7. Serve the **Green Tomato Salad** immediately as a refreshing side dish or appetizer.

Lush Vegetable Salad

Serves: 4 | Prep & Cook time: 20 Min

- 200g cherry tomatoes, halved
- 1 large cucumber, diced
- 1 red bell pepper, diced
- 1 yellow bell pepper, diced
- 1 small red onion, thinly sliced
- 100g feta cheese, crumbled
- 50g pitted black olives
- 2 tablespoons extra virgin olive oil
- 1 tablespoon lemon juice
- 1 teaspoon dried oregano
- Salt and pepper to taste
- Fresh parsley, chopped (for garnish)

DIRECTIONS:

1. In a large mixing bowl, combine the cherry tomatoes, diced cucumber, diced red bell pepper, diced yellow bell pepper, and thinly sliced red onion.
2. In a small bowl, whisk together the extra virgin olive oil, lemon juice, dried oregano, salt, and pepper to make the dressing.
3. Pour the dressing over the vegetable mixture and toss gently to coat all the vegetables evenly.
4. Place the vegetable mixture in Zone 1 of the air fryer, spreading it out in a single layer.
5. Select Zone 1, choose the AIR FRY function, and set the temperature to 180°C. Set the cooking time to 8 minutes (until the vegetables are slightly softened and lightly charred). Press the START/STOP.
6. Once cooked, remove the vegetable mixture from the air fryer and let it cool for a few minutes.
7. Transfer the vegetable mixture to a serving dish and sprinkle crumbled feta cheese and black olives on top.
8. Garnish with fresh parsley and serve the **Lush Vegetable Salad** as a refreshing and nutritious side dish or light lunch.

Corn & Coriander Salad

Serves: 2 | Prep & Cook time: 15 Min

- 2 ears of corn, husked
- 1 small red onion, finely chopped
- 1 small red bell pepper, finely chopped
- 1 small green bell pepper, finely chopped
- 4 tablespoons fresh coriander (cilantro), chopped
- 2 tablespoons lime juice
- 2 tablespoons extra virgin olive oil
- Salt and pepper to taste.

DIRECTIONS:

1. Place the corn ears in Zone 1. Select Zone 1, choose the ROAST function, and set the temperature to 200°C, time to 8 minutes or until the corn kernels are tender and slightly charred.
2. Turn the corn ears halfway through cooking for even browning.
3. Once cooked, remove the corn ears from the air fryer and let them cool slightly.
4. Using a sharp knife, carefully cut the kernels off the cobs and transfer them to a large mixing bowl.
5. Add the chopped red onion, red bell pepper, green bell pepper, and fresh coriander to the bowl with the corn kernels.
6. In a separate small bowl, whisk together the lime juice, extra virgin olive oil, salt, and pepper to make the dressing.
7. Pour the dressing over the corn and vegetable mixture and toss gently to coat everything evenly.
8. Let the salad marinate for a few minutes to allow the flavors to meld together.
9. Serve the **Corn and Coriander Salad** as a refreshing side dish or light lunch option.

Traditional Queso Fundido

Serves: 4 | Prep & Cook time: 20 Min

- 200g grated Cheddar cheese
- 200g grated Monterey Jack cheese
- 1 tablespoon olive oil
- 1 small onion, finely chopped
- 2 cloves garlic, minced
- 1 jalapeno pepper, seeded and finely chopped (optional)
- 1/2 teaspoon ground cumin
- 1/2 teaspoon paprika
- Salt and pepper, to taste
- Tortilla chips, for serving

DIRECTIONS:

1. In a skillet, heat the vegetable oil over medium heat. Add the diced onion and jalapeño pepper (if using) and sauté until softened, about 3-4 minutes. Add the minced garlic to the skillet and sauté for an additional minute.
2. Add the diced tomatoes to the skillet and cook for 2-3 minutes, stirring occasionally, until the tomatoes are heated through.
3. In Zone 1, place the grated Cheddar cheese and Monterey Jack cheese in an even layer.
4. Insert the air fryer basket into Air Fryer. Select Zone 1, choosing AIR FRY and setting the temperature to 180°C in 5 minutes. This will melt the cheese and create a gooey base.
5. After 5 minutes, carefully remove the air fryer basket and top the melted cheese with the sautéed onion, jalapeño, garlic, and diced tomatoes.
6. Return the air fryer basket to Zone 1 of the air fryer and continue cooking for an additional 5 minutes or until the cheese is fully melted and bubbling.
7. Once done, remove the air fryer basket from the Ninja Dual Zone Air Fryer and sprinkle the chopped fresh cilantro over the melted cheese.
8. Season with salt and pepper to taste.
9. Serve the **Traditional Queso Fundido** immediately with tortilla chips for dipping.

Beetroot Salad with Lemon Vinaigrette

Serves: 4 | Prep & Cook time: 35 Min

- 4 medium beetroots, peeled and sliced
- 100g mixed salad greens
- 50g crumbled feta cheese
- 2 tablespoons chopped fresh parsley

For the Lemon Vinaigrette:
- 2 tablespoons freshly squeezed lemon juice
- 4 tablespoons extra virgin olive oil
- 1 teaspoon Dijon mustard
- Salt and pepper to taste

DIRECTIONS:

1. In Zone 1 of the air fryer basket, place the sliced beetroots in a single layer. You may need to cook them in two zone depending on the size of your air fryer.
2. Select Zone 1, choose the AIR FRY, temperature :180°C in 15-20 minutes or until they are tender when pierced with a fork. (Select MACTH if cook in both zone)
3. While the beetroots are cooking, prepare the lemon vinaigrette. In a small bowl, whisk together the lemon juice, olive oil, Dijon mustard, salt, and pepper until well combined. Set aside.
4. Once the beetroots are cooked, remove the air fryer basket from Zone 1 and let the beetroots cool for a few minutes.
5. In a large bowl, combine the mixed salad greens and the air-fried beetroot slices. Drizzle the lemon vinaigrette over the salad and toss gently to coat.
6. Sprinkle the crumbled feta cheese and chopped fresh parsley over the salad.
7. Serve the **Beetroot Salad with Lemon Vinaigrette** immediately as a refreshing and vibrant side dish.

Purple Potato Chips with Rosemary

Serves: 4 | Prep & Cook time: 25 Min

- 500g purple potatoes
- 2 tablespoons olive oil
- 1 tablespoon chopped fresh rosemary
- Salt to taste

DIRECTIONS:

1. Wash and scrub the purple potatoes thoroughly to remove any dirt. Leave the skin on for added color and texture. Slice the potatoes into thin, even rounds using a mandoline or a sharp knife.
2. In a large bowl, toss the potato slices with olive oil, chopped fresh rosemary, and salt. Make sure each slice is well coated with the oil and seasoning.
3. Place a single layer of the seasoned potato slices in both zone of the air fryer. Select zone 1, select AIR FRY and set temperature to 180°C and set time to 15 minutes. Select MATCH to duplicate settings across both zones. Press the START/STOP button to begin cooking.
4. Once the cooking time is complete, remove the basket from the Air Fryer and let the chips cool for a few minutes. They will continue to crisp up as they cool down.
5. Serve the **Purple Potato Chips with Rosemary** as a tasty and colorful snack or as a side dish to complement your meals.

Baked Cheese Sandwich

Serves: 2 | Prep & Cook time: 20 Min

- 4 slices of bread (white, whole wheat, or your preferred choice)
- Butter, softened, for spreading
- 100g cheddar cheese, grated
- 50g mozzarella cheese, grated
- 2 tablespoons mayonnaise
- 1 teaspoon Dijon mustard
- Salt and pepper to taste
- Optional toppings: sliced tomatoes, cooked bacon, ham, or any other desired fillings

DIRECTIONS:

1. In a small bowl, mix together the grated cheddar cheese and mozzarella cheese.
2. In another bowl, combine the mayonnaise and Dijon mustard. Season with salt and pepper to taste.
3. Spread butter on one side of each bread slice. Place two slices, buttered side down, in Zone 1 of the air fryer basket.
4. Spread the mayonnaise and mustard mixture evenly on the non-buttered side of the bread slices.
5. Sprinkle the cheese mixture on top of the mayonnaise-mustard mixture. Add any desired toppings, such as sliced tomatoes, cooked bacon, or ham.
6. Place the remaining two slices of bread on top, buttered side up. Then place them in basket of zone 1.
7. Select zone 1, select BAKE, set temperature to 180°C and set time to 10 minutes. Press the START/STOP button to begin cooking.
8. After 5 minutes, carefully flip the sandwich using a spatula or tongs to ensure even browning on both sides.
9. Continue cooking for the remaining 5 minutes or until the bread turns golden brown and the cheese is melted and gooey.
10. Once cooked, remove the **Baked Cheese Sandwich** from the Ninja Dual Zone Air Fryer and let it cool for a few minutes before slicing and serving.
11. Serve the Baked Cheese Sandwich as a delicious and satisfying meal or snack.

Butter & Garlic Fried Cabbage

Serves: 2 | Prep & Cook time: 20 Min

- 1/2 small cabbage head, thinly sliced
- 2 tablespoons butter
- 2 cloves garlic, minced
- 1/2 teaspoon salt
- 1/4 teaspoon black pepper
- 1/4 teaspoon paprika (optional)

DIRECTIONS:

1. In a large bowl, toss the sliced cabbage with salt, black pepper, and paprika (if using).
2. Place the butter in Zone 1 of the Ninja Dual Zone Air Fryer and let it melt. (about 1 minutes)
3. Add the minced garlic to the melted butter and sauté for 2 minute, until fragrant.
4. Add the seasoned cabbage to the air fryer basket in Zone 1. Close Zone 1.
5. Select Zone 1, choose the AIR FRY function, and set the temperature to 180°C. Set the cooking time to 12 minutes. Press the START/STOP button to begin air frying.
6. Every 4 minutes, open Zone 1 and give the cabbage a stir to ensure even cooking.
7. After 12 minutes of cooking, check the cabbage for desired tenderness. If needed, continue cooking for an additional 2-3 minutes.
8. Once cooked to your liking, remove the **butter and garlic fried cabbage** from the air fryer and serve it hot.

Lebanese Baba Ghanoush

Serves: 4 | Prep & Cook time: 40 Min

- 2 large aubergines (eggplants)
- 2 garlic cloves, minced
- 3 tablespoons tahini
- 2 tablespoons freshly squeezed lemon juice
- 2 tablespoons extra-virgin olive oil
- 1/2 teaspoon ground cumin
- Salt, to taste
- Fresh parsley, for garnish
- Extra olive oil, for drizzling.

DIRECTIONS:

1. Using a fork, prick the aubergines all over. This will allow steam to escape during cooking and prevent them from bursting.
2. Place the aubergines in the zone 1 basket, choose ROAST function, temperature to 200°C and cooking time to 25 minutes or until the skin is charred and the flesh is soft and cooked through.
3. Flip them halfway through cooking for even browning.
4. Remove the cooked aubergines from air fryer and let them cool slightly. Once cool enough to handle, cut the aubergines in half lengthwise and scoop out the flesh using a spoon. Discard the charred skin.
5. Place the aubergine flesh in a colander or sieve to drain excess liquid for about 10 minutes.
6. In a food processor, combine the drained aubergine, minced garlic, tahini, lemon juice, olive oil, ground cumin, and salt. Pulse until well blended and creamy. Taste and adjust the seasonings if needed.
7. Transfer the Baba Ghanoush to a serving dish. Garnish with fresh parsley and drizzle with some extra olive oil.
8. Serve the **Lebanese Baba Ghanoush** with pita bread, crackers, or fresh vegetables for dipping.

Cheesy Baked Grits

Serves: 6 | Prep & Cook time: 40 Min

- 160g grits
- 950ml water
- 1 teaspoon salt
- 200g grated cheddar cheese
- 30g grated Parmesan cheese
- 30g butter
- 120ml milk
- 2 large eggs, beaten
- 1/2 teaspoon garlic powder
- Salt and pepper to taste
- Chopped fresh parsley (for garnish)

DIRECTIONS:

1. In a saucepan, bring the water to a boil. Add the salt and slowly whisk in the grits. Reduce the heat to low and simmer for about 5 minutes, stirring occasionally, until the grits are thickened.
2. Stir in the grated cheddar cheese, Parmesan cheese, butter, milk, garlic powder, salt, and pepper into the cooked grits until the cheese is melted and the mixture is well combined.
3. Remove the saucepan from the heat and let it cool for a few minutes. Stir in the beaten eggs until fully incorporated.
4. In Zone 1 of the air fryer basket, pour the cheesy grits mixture. Place the basket in the Air Fryer.
5. Select Zone 1, then choosing the BAKE program and setting the temperature to 180°C in 30 minutes until the top is golden and the edges are slightly crisp.
6. Once the cooking time is complete, remove the air fryer basket and let it cool for a few minutes.
7. Garnish with chopped fresh parsley and serve the **Cheesy Baked Grits** hot.

Beery & Crunchy Onion Rings

Serves: 4 | Prep & Cook time: 25 Min

- 2 large onions
- 200g all-purpose flour
- 1 teaspoon paprika
- 1/2 teaspoon garlic powder
- 1/4 teaspoon black pepper
- 250ml beer (preferably a light lager)
- Vegetable oil, for frying
- 1/2 teaspoon salt
- Dipping sauce of your choice (e.g., ketchup, mayo, BBQ sauce)

DIRECTIONS:

1. Peel the onions and slice them into thick rings. Separate the rings and set them aside.
2. In a mixing bowl, combine the flour, paprika, garlic powder, salt, and black pepper. Whisk until well combined.
3. Gradually pour the beer into the flour mixture, whisking continuously, until you have a smooth batter with a thick consistency.
4. Dip each onion ring into the batter, ensuring it is fully coated, and then let any excess batter drip off.
5. Place the coated onion rings in a single layer in both Zone of air Fryer.
6. Select zone 1, select AIR FRY and set temperature to 200°C and set time to 10 minutes. Select MATCH to duplicate settings across both zones. Press the START/STOP button to begin cooking.
7. Near the end of the cooking time, check the onions for golden brown and crispy. If not, cook for another 3-5 minutes.
8. Once the onion rings are cooked, remove them from the air fryer and transfer to a paper towel-lined plate to drain any excess oil.
9. Serve the **Beery and Crunchy Onion Rings** hot with your favorite dipping sauce.

Air Fried Courgette Sticks

Serves: 4 | Prep & Cook time: 25 Min

- 2 medium courgettes (zucchini)
- 2 large eggs, beaten
- 100g breadcrumbs
- 50g grated Parmesan cheese
- 1 teaspoon dried mixed herbs
- 1/2 teaspoon garlic powder
- 1/4 teaspoon black pepper
- 1/2 teaspoon salt
- Cooking spray or olive oil, for greasing.

DIRECTIONS:

1. Wash the courgettes and cut them into sticks, approximately 1 cm thick and 7-8 cm long. Set aside.
2. In a shallow dish, combine the breadcrumbs, grated Parmesan cheese, dried mixed herbs, garlic powder, salt, and black pepper. Mix well.
3. Dip each courgette stick into the beaten eggs, allowing any excess to drip off.
4. Roll the egg-coated courgette stick in the breadcrumb mixture, pressing lightly to ensure it is evenly coated. Repeat with the remaining courgette sticks.
5. Lightly grease the air fryer basket with cooking spray or a small amount of olive oil to prevent sticking.
6. In Zone 1 of the air fryer basket, place the coated courgette sticks in a single layer. You may need to cook them in two zone depending on the size of your air fryer.
7. Select Zone 1, choosing AIR FRY and setting the temperature to 200°C in10 minutes. Check them until the courgette sticks are golden brown and crispy.
8. Once the courgette sticks are cooked, remove them from the air fryer and transfer to a serving plate
9. Serve the **Air Fried Courgette Sticks** hot as a delicious appetizer or side dish. They can be enjoyed on their own or with a dipping sauce of your choice, such as marinara sauce or tzatziki.

Easy Croutons

Serves: 4 | Prep & Cook time: 12 Min

- 4 slices of bread (white or wholemeal)
- 2 tablespoons olive oil
- 1 teaspoon dried herbs (such as thyme, oregano, or Italian seasoning)
- 1/2 teaspoon garlic powder (optional)
- Salt and pepper to taste.

DIRECTIONS:

1. Cut the bread slices into small cubes or bite-sized pieces.
2. In a bowl, combine the olive oil, dried herbs, salt, and pepper. Mix well.
3. Add the bread cubes to the bowl and toss them gently to coat them evenly with the seasoned oil mixture.
4. Place the seasoned bread cubes in Zone 1 of the air fryer basket, ensuring they are in a single layer for even cooking.
5. Insert the air fryer basket into air fryer zone 1. Select Zone 1, choosing AIR FRY, set the temperature to 180°C, set the cooking time to 7 minutes. Keep an eye on the croutons and shake the basket or stir them occasionally for even browning. Check them periodically to avoid burning.
6. Once the croutons are done, remove them from the air fryer and let them cool slightly before using or storing.
7. Serve the **Easy Croutons** as a crunchy topping for salads, soups, or as a delicious snack on their own.

Buffalo Cauliflower with Blue Cheese

Serves: 6 | Prep & Cook time: 30 Min

- 1 large head of cauliflower, cut into florets
- 125g plain flour
- 1 teaspoon garlic powder
- 1 teaspoon onion powder
- 1/2 teaspoon paprika
- 1/2 teaspoon salt
- 1/4 teaspoon black pepper
- 240ml milk (or plant-based milk for a vegan version)
- 120ml hot sauce (such as Frank's RedHot)
- 60g crumbled blue cheese (or dairy-free blue cheese for a vegan version)
- 60g melted butter (or vegan butter for a vegan version)
- Fresh parsley, chopped (for garnish).

DIRECTIONS

1. In a large mixing bowl, combine the flour, garlic powder, onion powder, paprika, salt, and black pepper.
2. Dip each cauliflower floret into the milk, then roll it in the flour mixture until evenly coated. Shake off any excess flour.
3. Place the coated cauliflower florets in Zone 1 of the air fryer basket in a single layer. (if overcrowded, put the rest to zone 2 and cook on both zones).
4. Select Zone 1, choose the AIR FRY, and set the temperature to 200°C. Set the time to 15 minutes (or until the cauliflower is crispy and golden brown). Press the START/STOP.
5. Shake the basket halfway through cooking for even browning.
6. While the cauliflower is cooking, prepare the buffalo sauce. In a small saucepan, heat the hot sauce and melted butter over low heat until well combined.
7. Once the cauliflower is cooked, transfer it to a large mixing bowl. Pour the buffalo sauce over the cauliflower and toss to coat evenly.
8. Return the coated cauliflower to the air fryer basket in Zone 1. choose the AIR FRY, and set the temperature to 200°C, cook for an additional 5 minutes to allow the sauce to adhere and the flavors to meld.
9. Remove the buffalo cauliflower from the air fryer and sprinkle the crumbled blue cheese over the top.
10. Garnish with fresh parsley and serve hot as a delicious appetizer or side dish.
11. This **Buffalo Cauliflower with Blue Cheese** recipe offers a tasty twist on traditional buffalo wings, The crispy cauliflower florets are coated in a spicy buffalo sauce and topped with tangy blue cheese crumbles. Enjoy!

Dinner Rolls

Serves: 6 | Prep & Cook time: 30 Min

- 450g strong white bread flour
- 1 teaspoon salt
- 2 tablespoons granulated sugar
- 7g sachet fast-action dried yeast
- 250ml warm milk
- 50g unsalted butter, melted
- Olive oil, for greasing
- Egg wash (1 beaten egg mixed with 1 tablespoon milk), for brushing.

DIRECTIONS

1. In a large mixing bowl, combine the bread flour, salt, and sugar. Make a well in the center.
2. In a separate bowl, mix the dried yeast with warm milk and let it sit for a few minutes until it becomes frothy.
3. Pour the yeast mixture into the well of the dry ingredients. Add the melted butter.
4. Stir the mixture with a wooden spoon until it starts to come together, then use your hands to knead the dough in the bowl until it forms a smooth and elastic dough. You can also use a stand mixer with a dough hook attachment for this step.
5. Lightly flour a clean surface and turn out the dough onto it. Knead the dough for about 10 minutes until it becomes soft and elastic.
6. Grease a clean bowl with olive oil and place the dough in it. Cover the bowl with a clean kitchen towel or plastic wrap. Let the dough rise in a warm place for about 1 hour or until it has doubled in size.
7. After the dough has risen, gently punch it down to release any air bubbles. Transfer the dough onto a lightly floured surface.
8. Divide the dough into 6 equal portions. Shape each portion into a smooth ball by tucking the edges underneath.
9. Grease the air fryer basket in Zone 1 of the Ninja Dual Zone Air Fryer with olive oil. Place the shaped dough balls in a single layer in the greased basket, leaving space between them for expansion. Brush the tops of the dough balls with the egg wash.
10. Select Zone 1, choose the BAKE function, and set the temperature to 180°C. Set the cooking time to 10 minutes. Press the START/STOP button to begin baking.
11. Once the cooking time is complete, remove the Dinner Rolls from the air fryer and let them cool on a wire rack.
12. Serve the warm and freshly baked **Dinner Rolls** as a delightful addition to your meal.

Crispy Lemon Artichoke Hearts

Serves: 2 | Prep & Cook time: 25 Min

- 1 can of artichoke hearts in water (400g), drained and rinsed
- 1 egg, beaten
- 2 tablespoons plain flour
- 1/4 teaspoon garlic powder
- 1/4 teaspoon lemon zest
- 1/4 teaspoon dried thyme
- 1/4 teaspoon salt
- 1/8 teaspoon black pepper
- 60g breadcrumbs
- Cooking spray or oil, for greasing.

DIRECTIONS

1. Pat dry the drained and rinsed artichoke hearts using a clean kitchen towel or paper towels.
2. In a shallow dish, combine the flour, garlic powder, lemon zest, dried thyme, salt, and black pepper. Mix well.
3. Dip each artichoke heart into the beaten egg, allowing any excess to drip off.
4. Coat the dipped artichoke hearts with the flour mixture, ensuring they are evenly coated.
5. In another shallow dish, place the breadcrumbs.
6. Roll the coated artichoke hearts in the breadcrumbs, pressing gently to adhere the breadcrumbs to the surface.
7. Lightly grease the cooking basket in Zone 1 of the Ninja Dual Zone Air Fryer with cooking spray or a small amount of oil.
8. Place the breaded artichoke hearts in Zone 1's cooking basket in a single layer, ensuring they do not overlap.
9. Select Zone 1, choose the AIR FRY, temperature to 200°C, cooking time to 12-15 minutes.
10. Halfway through the cooking time, pause the air fryer and shake the basket to ensure even browning. Then, continue cooking until the artichoke hearts are golden brown and crispy.
11. Once the cooking time is complete, carefully remove the basket from the air fryer and let the crispy lemon artichoke hearts cool for a few minutes.
12. Serve the **Crispy Lemon Artichoke Hearts** as a delicious appetizer or side dish. They can be enjoyed as is or with a dipping sauce of your choice.

Cheddar Quiche

Serves: 4 | Prep & Cook time: 40 Min

- 4 large eggs
- 200ml milk
- 200g shortcrust pastry
- 150g grated cheddar cheese
- 100g diced cooked bacon or ham
- 1/2 teaspoon dried thyme
- Salt and pepper to taste
- Cooking spray or oil for greasing.

DIRECTIONS:

1. Roll out the shortcrust pastry on a lightly floured surface and line a greased pie dish that fits in Zone 1.
2. Prick the pastry base with a fork and blind bake it for 10 minutes in the preheated air fryer.
3. In a mixing bowl, whisk together the eggs, milk, dried thyme, salt, and pepper until well combined.
4. Sprinkle the grated cheddar cheese and diced cooked bacon or ham over the partially baked pastry base.
5. Pour the egg mixture over the cheese and bacon or ham.
6. Place the quiche in Zone 1 of the Ninja Dual Zone Air Fryer.
7. Select Zone 1, choose the BAKE program, and set the temperature to 180°C. Set the time to 20-25 minutes.
8. Press the START/STOP button to begin cooking.
9. Check the quiche after 20 minutes by inserting a toothpick into the center. If it comes out clean, it is done. If not, continue cooking for an additional 3-5 minutes.
10. Once cooked, carefully remove the **quiche** from the air fryer and let it cool for a few minutes before serving.

Air Fryer Chicken Wings

Serves: 2 | Prep & Cook time: 35 Min

- 500g chicken wings
- 2 tablespoons olive oil
- 1 teaspoon paprika
- 1 teaspoon garlic powder
- 1/2 teaspoon salt
- 1/4 teaspoon black pepper
- Your choice of dipping sauce (e.g., BBQ sauce, ranch dressing)

DIRECTIONS:

1. In a large bowl, combine the olive oil, paprika, garlic powder, salt, and black pepper. Mix well.
2. Add the chicken wings to the bowl and toss them in the seasoning mixture until they are evenly coated.
3. Lightly grease Zone 1 of the air fryer with cooking spray or a small amount of oil.
4. Place the chicken wings in Zone 1, making sure they are in a single layer and not touching each other.
5. Select Zone 1, choose the AIR FRY program, and set the temperature to 200°C. Set the time to 20-25 minutes.
6. Press the START/STOP button to begin cooking.
7. After 10 minutes of cooking, pause the air fryer, open it, and carefully flip the chicken wings.
8. Close the air fryer and resume cooking for the remaining time or until the chicken wings are golden brown and cooked through.
9. Once cooked, remove the chicken wings from the air fryer and let them rest for a few minutes.
10. Serve the **air fryer chicken wings** hot with your favorite dipping sauce. They are delicious on their own or paired with celery sticks and a side of fries.

Chapter 3: Family's Favorites Dishes

BBQ Chicken & Chips

Serves: 4 | Prep & Cook time: 30 Min

- 4 large eggs
- 60ml milk
- 50g grated cheddar cheese
- 50g diced cooked ham
- 50g diced bell peppers
- 50g diced onion
- Salt and pepper to taste
- Cooking spray or oil for greasing.

DIRECTIONS:

1. Soak cut potatoes in cold water for 30 minutes to remove excess starch. Drain well, then pat with a paper towel until very dry.
2. Meanwhile, roll chicken breasts into a neat shape and wrap with bacon. Secure in place with a cocktail stick.
3. Place chips with oil into a large mixing bowl; toss to combine with at least ½ tablespoon oil. For crispier results, use up to 3 tablespoons oil.
4. Insert a crisper plate in both drawers. Place chicken breasts in zone 1, then insert drawer in unit. Place fries in zone 2, then insert drawer in unit.
5. Select zone 1, select ROAST, set temperature to 180°C and set time to 25 minutes.
6. Select zone 2, select AIR FRY, set temperature to 200°C, and set time to 25 minutes. Select SYNC. Select START/ STOP.
7. When zone 1 time reaches 10 minutes, remove drawer from unit and top chicken with cheese. Reinsert drawer to continue cooking.
8. When zone 2 time reaches 10 minutes, remove drawer from unit and shake drawer for 10 seconds. Reinsert drawer to continue cooking.
9. When zone 2 time reaches 20 minutes, shake for 10 seconds. Sprinkle with sea salt to serve.
10. Cooking is complete when their internal temperature reaches at least 75°C on an instant-read thermometer. Serve **chicken drizzled with BBQ sauce and chips**.

Cheesy Quesadillas with Salsa

Serves: 5 | Prep & Cook time: 30 Min

- 100g grated cheddar cheese
- 100g smoked Gouda, rind removed and grated
- 2 spring onions, sliced thinly
- 40g sliced black olives
- 40g pepperdew peppers
- 5g fresh coriander, roughly chopped
- 10 mini flour tortillas (approx.12 cm)
- 100g cream cheese
- Cooking oil spray.

To Serve:
- Ready-made salsa and guacamole
- Sour cream
- Hot sauce.

DIRECTIONS:

1. In a large mixing bowl, combine cheddar, Gouda, onions, olives, pepperdew peppers and coriander together.
2. Spread tortillas out on clean work surface, spray oil on one side and flip. Evenly spread 1 tablespoon cream cheese on each tortilla.
3. Evenly spread the cheese mixture on five tortillas, then cover cheese like a sandwich with remaining five tortillas with the cheese spread facing inwards. Press down.
4. Place one quesadilla in each drawer. Select zone 1, select AIR FRY, set temperature to 200°C, and set time for 15 minutes. Select MATCH to duplicate settings across both zones. Select START/STOP to begin cooking. After 2 minutes flip over with silicone coated tongs and reinsert drawers to continue cooking. Cook for 2-3 more minutes and remove carefully with tongs. Proceed with remaining three quesadillas tortillas until all are cooked for 4-5 minutes each.
5. When cooking is complete, slice **quesadillas** into wedges and serve with salsa, guacamole and sour cream and liberal dash of hot sauce.

Fish & Vegetable Tacos

Serves: 4 | Prep & Cook time: 30 Min

- 4 white fish fillets (such as cod or haddock), about 150g each
- 2 tablespoons olive oil
- 1 tablespoon lime juice
- 1 teaspoon ground cumin
- 1 teaspoon paprika
- 1/2 teaspoon garlic powder
- 1/2 teaspoon chili powder
- Salt and pepper to taste
- 8 small flour tortillas
- 100g shredded lettuce
- 150g sliced bell peppers
- 75g sliced red onion
- Fresh cilantro leaves (for garnish)
- Lime wedges (for serving)

DIRECTIONS:

1. In a bowl, combine the olive oil, lime juice, cumin, paprika, garlic powder, chili powder, salt, and pepper to create a marinade.
2. Place the fish fillets in the marinade and ensure they are coated evenly. Allow the fish to marinate for about 10 minutes.
3. While the fish is marinating, prepare the vegetables by slicing the bell peppers and red onion.
4. Place the marinated fish fillets, sliced bell peppers, and red onion in the cooking basket of one zone.
5. Select the "AIR FRY" program. Set the temperature to 200°C and set the cooking time to 15 minutes. Press START/STOP to begin cooking.
6. While the fish and vegetables are cooking, warm the flour tortillas according to package instructions or your preference.
7. Once the fish and vegetables are cooked, carefully remove them from the air fryer and let them cool for a few minutes. Flake the fish into smaller pieces.
8. Assemble the tacos by placing a generous amount of shredded lettuce, flaked fish, sliced bell peppers, and red onion on each tortilla.
9. Garnish with fresh cilantro leaves and serve with lime wedges on the side.
10. Enjoy your delicious **Fish and Vegetable Tacos**!

Pork Stuffing Meatballs

Serves: 30 meatballs | Prep & Cook time: 20 Min

- 500g ground pork
- 150g breadcrumbs
- 1 small onion, finely chopped
- 2 cloves of garlic, minced
- 2 tablespoons fresh parsley, chopped
- 1 tablespoon fresh sage, chopped
- 1 tablespoon fresh thyme, chopped
- 1 teaspoon salt
- 1/2 teaspoon black pepper
- 2 large eggs, beaten
- 30g butter, melted

DIRECTIONS:

1. In a large mixing bowl, combine the pork mince, breadcrumbs, chopped onion, minced garlic, chopped parsley, chopped sage, chopped thyme, salt, and black pepper. Mix well.
2. Add the beaten eggs to the mixture and mix until everything is evenly combined.
3. Shape the mixture into small meatballs, about the size of a golf ball, and place them on a baking sheet or tray lined with parchment paper. Evenly dividing them between the two zone.
4. Insert the baking sheet with the meatballs into both zone of the Air Fryer and close the lid.
5. Select zone 1, select AIR FRY and set temperature to 180°C and set time to 15 minutes. Select MATCH to duplicate settings across both zones. Press the START/STOP button to begin cooking.
6. While the meatballs are cooking, melt the butter in a small saucepan or microwave-safe dish.
7. When the meatballs are cooked, remove them from the Air Fryer and brush them with the melted butter for added flavor and moisture.
8. Serve the **pork stuffing meatballs** hot as an appetizer or main dish. They can be enjoyed on their own or served with a side of cranberry sauce or gravy.

Fried Green Tomatoes

Serves: 4 | Prep & Cook time: 30 Min

- 4 green tomatoes, sliced into 6mm thick rounds
- 2 large eggs, beaten
- 120g all-purpose flour
- 1 teaspoon paprika
- 1/2 teaspoon garlic powder
- 1/2 teaspoon onion powder
- 1/4 teaspoon cayenne pepper (optional, for a spicy kick)
- Salt and pepper to taste
- 80g breadcrumbs
- Cooking spray.

DIRECTIONS:

1. In a shallow dish, combine the all-purpose flour, paprika, garlic powder, onion powder, cayenne pepper (if using), salt, and pepper. Mix well.
2. In another shallow dish, place the beaten eggs.
3. Place the breadcrumbs in a third shallow dish.
4. Dip each tomato slice into the flour mixture, coating both sides. Shake off any excess flour.
5. Dip the floured tomato slice into the beaten eggs, ensuring both sides are coated.
6. Finally, dip the tomato slice into the breadcrumbs, pressing gently to adhere the crumbs to the tomato.
7. Repeat the breading process for the remaining tomato slices.
8. Lightly coat the air fryer basket of both zone with cooking spray.
9. Place the breaded tomato slices in a single layer in two zone of the air fryer.
10. Select Zone 1, choose AIR FRY, set the temperature to 200°C, and set the time to 15 minutes. Select MATCH to duplicate settings across both zones. Press the START/STOP button to begin cooking.
11. Serve the **fried green tomatoes** hot as an appetizer or side dish. They are delicious on their own or served with a dipping sauce of your choice.

Chinese-Inspired Spareribs

Serves: 4 | Prep & Cook time: 25 Min

- 800g pork spareribs
- 2 cloves garlic, minced
- 2 tablespoons soy sauce
- 2 tablespoons hoisin sauce
- 2 tablespoons honey
- 1 tablespoon rice vinegar
- 1 teaspoon ginger, grated
- 1/2 teaspoon Chinese five-spice powder
- 1/4 teaspoon black pepper
- Optional garnish: chopped spring onions

DIRECTIONS:

1. In a bowl, combine the soy sauce, hoisin sauce, honey, rice vinegar, minced garlic, grated ginger, Chinese five-spice powder, and black pepper. Mix well to make the marinade.
2. Place the spareribs in a large ziplock bag or a shallow dish and pour the marinade over them. Ensure the ribs are well coated. Marinate for at least 2 hours or overnight in the refrigerator for best results.
3. Lightly coat the air fryer basket of both zone with cooking spray.
4. Evenly dividing the marinated spareribs between the two zone. Place them in a single layer in both zone of the air fryer, reserving any leftover marinade.
5. Select Zone 1, choose the AIR FRY program, set the temperature to 180°C, and set the time to 28 minutes. Select MATCH. Press the START/STOP.
6. While the spareribs are cooking, pour the reserved marinade into a small saucepan and bring it to a simmer. Let it cook for a few minutes until it thickens slightly, stirring occasionally. This will be used as a glaze for the cooked spareribs.
7. After the cooking time, carefully remove the spareribs and brush them with the glaze on both sides.
8. Once all the spareribs are cooked and glazed, garnish them with chopped spring onions if desired.
9. Serve the **Chinese-inspired spareribs** hot as a main dish. They can be enjoyed on their own or served with steamed rice and stir-fried vegetables.

Cajun Shrimp

Serves: 4 | Prep & Cook time: 30 Min

- 450g large shrimp, peeled and deveined
- 2 tablespoons olive oil
- 1 tablespoon Cajun seasoning
- 1 teaspoon paprika
- 1 teaspoon garlic powder
- 1/4 teaspoon black pepper
- 1/4 teaspoon cayenne pepper (adjust to taste)
- 1 tablespoon fresh lemon juice
- Chopped fresh parsley (for garnish)
- Lemon wedges (for serving)
- 1/2 teaspoon salt

DIRECTIONS:

1. In a large bowl, combine the olive oil, Cajun seasoning, paprika, garlic powder, salt, black pepper, cayenne pepper, and lemon juice. Mix well to create a marinade.
2. Add the shrimp to the marinade and toss until they are evenly coated. Allow the shrimp to marinate for about 15-20 minutes.
3. Place the marinated shrimp in the cooking basket of one zone.
4. Select the "AIR FRY" program. Set the temperature to 200°C. Set the cooking time to 8 minutes. Press START/STOP to begin cooking. Shake the basket halfway through cooking to ensure even cooking.
5. While the shrimp are cooking, you can prepare a side dish or salad to accompany the meal.
6. Once the shrimp are cooked, remove them from the air fryer and transfer them to a serving dish.
7. Garnish with chopped fresh parsley and serve with lemon wedges on the side for squeezing over the shrimp.
8. Enjoy your delicious **Cajun Shrimp**!

Veggie Tuna Melts

Serves: 4 | Prep & Cook time: 25 Min

- 2 cans (320g total) tuna, drained
- 100g grated cheddar cheese
- 60g mayonnaise
- 40g finely chopped red onion
- 40g finely chopped celery
- 2 tablespoons chopped fresh parsley
- 1 tablespoon lemon juice
- Salt and pepper to taste
- 4 English muffins, split
- Butter for spreading
- Sliced tomato (optional)
- Sliced cucumber (optional)

DIRECTIONS:

1. In a mixing bowl, combine the drained tuna, grated cheddar cheese, mayonnaise, red onion, celery, parsley, lemon juice, salt, and pepper. Mix well to combine.
2. Spread butter on the cut sides of the English muffins.
3. Place the English muffins in one zone of the air fryer, cut-side up.
4. Select the "AIR FRY" program. Set the temperature to 180°C and set the cooking time to 4 minutes. Press START/STOP to begin cooking.
5. While the English muffins are toasting, spoon the tuna mixture evenly onto the cut sides of the muffins.
6. If desired, add sliced tomato and cucumber on top of the tuna mixture.
7. Once the English muffins are toasted, carefully remove them from the air fryer and place them on a serving plate.
8. Return the loaded English muffins to the air fryer basket, with the tuna side facing up.
9. Select "AIR FRY". Set the cooking time to 4 minutes. Set the temperature to 180°C. Press START/STOP.
10. Cook until the cheese is melted, and the tuna mixture is heated through.
11. Once cooked, remove the Veggie Tuna Melts from the air fryer and serve hot.
12. Enjoy your delicious **Veggie Tuna Melts**!

Coconut Chicken Tenders

Serves: 4 | Prep & Cook time: 25 Min

- 500g chicken tenders
- 2 eggs, beaten
- 100g shredded coconut
- 50g breadcrumbs
- 30g all-purpose flour
- 1/2 teaspoon salt
- 1/2 teaspoon paprika
- Cooking spray.

DIRECTIONS:

1. In a shallow bowl, combine the shredded coconut, breadcrumbs, salt, and paprika.
2. Place the flour in a separate shallow bowl.
3. Dip each chicken tender into the flour, shaking off any excess.
4. Dip the floured chicken tender into the beaten eggs, allowing any excess to drip off.
5. Roll the chicken tender in the coconut mixture, pressing gently to adhere the coating.
6. Repeat the process for the remaining chicken tenders.
7. Lightly coat the air fryer basket of both zone with cooking spray. Evenly dividing coated chicken tenders between the two zone. Place a single layer in each zone.
8. Select Zone 1, choose AIR FRY, set the temperature to 180°C, and set the time to 14 minutes. Select MATCH to duplicate settings across both zones. Press the START/STOP button to begin cooking.
9. Check the basket while cooking and gently shake the basket to make sure the food is cooks evenly.
10. Serve the **coconut chicken tenders** hot with your favorite dipping sauce.

Note: The cooking time may vary depending on the thickness of the chicken tenders. Adjust the cooking time as needed.

Steak & Vegetable Kebabs

Serves: 4 | Prep & Cook time: 40 Min

- 500g sirloin steak, cut into 2cm cubes
- 1 red bell pepper, seeded and cut into chunks
- 1 green bell pepper, seeded and cut into chunks
- 1 red onion, cut into chunks
- 8 cherry tomatoes
- 2 tablespoons olive oil
- 2 cloves garlic, minced
- 1 tablespoon Worcestershire sauce
- 1 tablespoon balsamic vinegar
- 1 teaspoon dried oregano
- Salt and pepper to taste
- Wooden or metal skewers.

DIRECTIONS:

1. In a bowl, combine the olive oil, minced garlic, Worcestershire sauce, balsamic vinegar, dried oregano, salt, and pepper.
2. Add the cubed steak to the marinade and toss to coat. Let it marinate for 10 minutes.
3. Thread the marinated steak, bell peppers, red onion, and cherry tomatoes onto skewers, alternating between the ingredients.
4. Lightly coat the air fryer basket of both zone with cooking spray.
5. Evenly dividing and Place the kebabs in a single layer in each zone.
6. Select Zone 1, choose the AIR FRY program, set the temperature to 200°C, and set the time to 12-15 minutes for medium-rare to medium doneness, or adjust the cooking time based on your desired level of doneness. Select MATCH to duplicate settings across both zones. Press the START/STOP button to begin cooking.
7. Serve the **steak and vegetable kebabs** hot with your favorite dipping sauce or alongside a fresh salad.

Frittata

Serves: 2 | Prep & Cook time: 25 Min

- 4 large eggs
- 60ml milk
- 50g grated cheddar cheese
- 50g diced cooked ham
- 50g diced bell peppers
- 50g diced onion
- Salt and pepper to taste
- Cooking spray or oil for greasing.

DIRECTIONS:

1. In a mixing bowl, whisk together the eggs and milk until well combined.
2. Add the grated cheddar cheese, diced cooked ham, diced bell peppers, diced onion, salt, and pepper to the bowl. Stir to combine all the ingredients.
3. Lightly grease a small baking dish or cake pan that fits in Zone 1 with cooking spray or a small amount of oil.
4. Pour the frittata mixture into the greased dish, spreading it evenly.
5. Place the baking dish in Zone 1 of the Ninja Dual Zone Air Fryer.
6. Select Zone 1, choose the BAKE program, and set the temperature to 180°C. Set the time to 15-18 minutes.
7. Press the START/STOP button to begin cooking.
8. Check the frittata after 15 minutes by inserting a toothpick into the center. If it comes out clean, it is done. If not, continue cooking for an additional 2-3 minutes.
9. Once cooked, carefully remove the frittata from the air fryer and let it cool in the dish for a few minutes.
10. Cut the **frittata** into slices or wedges and serve warm.

Spicy Chicken Tenders

Serves: 6 | Prep & Cook time: 30 Min

- 500g chicken breast fillets, cut into tenders
- 150g breadcrumbs
- 50g grated Parmesan cheese
- 1 teaspoon paprika
- 1/2 teaspoon cayenne pepper
- 1/2 teaspoon garlic powder
- 1/2 teaspoon onion powder
- 1/2 teaspoon salt
- 1/4 teaspoon black pepper
- 2 large eggs, beaten
- Cooking spray or oil for greasing.

DIRECTIONS:

1. In a shallow bowl or plate, combine the breadcrumbs, grated Parmesan cheese, paprika, cayenne pepper, garlic powder, onion powder, salt, and black pepper.
2. Dip each chicken tender into the beaten eggs, allow any excess to drip off, and then coat it in the breadcrumb mixture.
3. Repeat the dipping and coating process for all the chicken tenders.
4. Lightly grease Zone 1 and Zone 2 of the air fryer with cooking spray or a small amount of oil.
5. Place half of the coated chicken tenders in Zone 1 and the other half in Zone 2 of the Ninja Dual Zone Air Fryer, making sure they are in a single layer and not touching each other.
6. Select Zone 1, choose the AIR FRY program, and set the temperature to 200°C. Set the time to 10-12 minutes.
7. Select MATCH to duplicate settings across both zones. Press START/STOP to begin cooking.
8. After 5 minutes of cooking, pause the air fryer, open it, and carefully flip the chicken tenders in both zones.
9. Close the air fryer and resume cooking until the chicken tenders are golden brown and cooked through.
10. Once cooked, remove the **chicken tenders** from the air fryer and Serve the spicy chicken tenders hot with your favorite dipping sauce or as a main dish with sides.

Easy Chicken Nachos

Serves: 8 | Prep & Cook time: 20 Min

- 400 grams tortilla chips
- 200 grams cooked chicken, shredded
- 100 grams grated cheddar cheese
- 100 grams grated mozzarella cheese
- 75 grams diced tomatoes
- 75 grams diced red onion
- 30 grams sliced jalapeños (optional)
- 15 grams chopped fresh coriander (cilantro)
- Sour cream and guacamole, for serving

DIRECTIONS:

1. In each zone, spread a layer of tortilla chips on the crisper plate, ensuring they are evenly distributed. Distribute half of the shredded chicken evenly over the tortilla chips.
2. Sprinkle both zones with a combination of cheddar and mozzarella cheese.
3. In Zone 1, select the AIR FRY function, set the temperature to 180°C, and set the time to 10 minutes. Press the MATCH. Press the START/STOP button to begin cooking.
4. While the nachos are cooking, prepare the toppings by dicing the tomatoes, red onion, and jalapeños (if using), and chopping the fresh coriander (cilantro).
5. Once the cooking time is complete, remove the drawers from the air fryer and let the nachos cool for a few minutes.
6. Sprinkle the diced tomatoes, red onion, jalapeños (if using), and fresh coriander evenly over both zones of the nachos.
7. Serve the **Easy Chicken Nachos** hot with sour cream and guacamole on the side.

Chapter 4: Poultry

Turkey Meatloaf

Serves: 4 | Prep & Cook time: 45 Min

- 500 grams ground turkey
- 60 grams breadcrumbs
- 40 grams finely chopped onion
- 40 grams finely chopped red bell pepper
- 40 grams grated carrot
- 60 ml milk
- 1 large egg, lightly beaten
- 2 tablespoons Worcestershire sauce
- 1 tablespoon tomato paste
- 1 teaspoon dried thyme
- 1 teaspoon dried oregano
- 1/2 teaspoon garlic powder
- 1/2 teaspoon salt
- 1/4 teaspoon black pepper
- 2 tablespoons ketchup (for topping)

DIRECTIONS:

1. In a large mixing bowl, combine the ground turkey, breadcrumbs, finely chopped onion, red bell pepper, grated carrot, milk, lightly beaten egg, Worcestershire sauce, tomato paste, dried thyme, dried oregano, garlic powder, salt, and black pepper. Mix well until all the ingredients are evenly incorporated.
2. Divide the meat mixture in half and shape each portion into a loaf shape.
3. In Zone 1, place one meatloaf in the center of the crisper plate.
4. In Zone 2, place the second meatloaf in the center of the crisper plate.
5. In Zone 1, select the AIR FRY function, set temperature to 180°C, and set the time to 30 minutes. Press the MATCH. Press the START/STOP button to begin cooking.
6. After 18 minutes of cooking, open the drawers and spread 1 tablespoon of ketchup evenly over the top of each meatloaf.
7. Close the drawers and continue cooking for the remaining time.
8. Once the cooking time is complete, remove the drawers from the air fryer and let the meatloaves rest for a few minutes.
9. Slice the **Turkey Meatloaf** into portions and serve hot.

African Merguez Meatballs

Serves: 4 | Prep & Cook time: 25 Min

- 500g ground poultry (such as chicken or turkey)
- 1 small onion, finely chopped
- 2 garlic cloves, minced
- 1 teaspoon ground cumin
- 1 teaspoon ground coriander
- 1 teaspoon paprika
- 1/2 teaspoon ground cinnamon
- 1/2 teaspoon cayenne pepper (adjust to taste)
- 1/4 teaspoon black pepper
- 2 tablespoons chopped fresh parsley
- 2 tablespoons chopped fresh cilantro
- 1/2 teaspoon salt
- 1 tablespoon olive oil

DIRECTIONS:

1. In a large bowl, combine the ground poultry, chopped onion, minced garlic, ground cumin, ground coriander, paprika, ground cinnamon, cayenne pepper, salt, black pepper, chopped parsley, and chopped cilantro. Mix well until all the ingredients are evenly incorporated.
2. Shape the mixture into small meatballs, about 1-2 inches in diameter.
3. In Zone 1, place the meatballs in a single layer on the crisper plates, ensuring they are not touching each other. select the AIR FRY function. Set the temperature to 180°C and the time to 12 minutes.
4. Drizzle the olive oil over the meatballs to help them brown and prevent sticking.
5. Press the START/STOP button to begin cooking.
6. After 5-6 minutes, open the drawer in Zone 1 and gently shake it to rotate the meatballs.
7. Close the drawer and continue cooking for another 5-6 minutes or until the meatballs are cooked through and nicely browned.
8. Once done, remove the **meatballs** from the air fryer and let them rest for a few minutes before serving.

Honey-Glazed Chicken Thighs

Serves: 4 | Prep & Cook time: 65 Min

- 8 chicken thighs, bone-in and skin-on
- 2 tablespoons olive oil
- 2 tablespoons honey
- 2 tablespoons soy sauce
- 2 cloves garlic, minced
- 1 teaspoon ground paprika
- 1/2 teaspoon dried thyme
- Salt and pepper to taste
- Fresh parsley, chopped (for garnish)

DIRECTIONS:

1. In a large bowl, whisk together the olive oil, honey, soy sauce, minced garlic, ground paprika, dried thyme, salt, and pepper to create the marinade.
2. Add the chicken thighs to the marinade, ensuring they are coated evenly. Cover the bowl and let the chicken marinate in the refrigerator for 30 minutes.
3. Once the chicken has marinated, remove it from the marinade, allowing any excess marinade to drip off.
4. Place 4 chicken thighs in each zone of the air fryer, making sure they are evenly spaced.
5. In Zone 1, select the AIR FRY function, set the temperature to 180°C, and set the time to 25 minutes. Press the MACTH. Press the START/STOP button to begin cooking.
6. After 15 minutes of cooking, open the drawers and brush the chicken thighs with any remaining marinade.
7. Close the drawers and continue cooking for the remaining time or until the chicken thighs are cooked through and golden brown.
8. Once the cooking time is complete, remove the chicken thighs from the air fryer and let them rest for a few minutes.
9. Garnish the **Honey-Glazed Chicken Thighs** with freshly chopped parsley.
10. Serve the chicken thighs hot with your choice of sides, such as roasted vegetables, rice, or salad.

Easy Cajun Chicken Drumsticks

Serves: 4 | Prep & Cook time: 40 Min

- 8 chicken drumsticks
- 2 tablespoons olive oil
- 1 tablespoon Cajun seasoning
- 1 teaspoon paprika
- 1 teaspoon garlic powder
- 1/4 teaspoon black pepper
- 1/2 teaspoon salt.

DIRECTIONS:

1. In a bowl, combine the olive oil, Cajun seasoning, paprika, garlic powder, salt, and black pepper. Mix well to create a marinade.
2. Place the chicken drumsticks in a shallow dish and coat them with the marinade, ensuring they are evenly coated.
3. Evenly dividing them between the two zone, place the chicken drumsticks on the crisper plates.
4. In Zone 1, Select the AIR FRY function, set the temperature to 190°C, and set the time to 25-30 minutes. Select MATCH to duplicate settings across both zones. Press the START/STOP button to begin cooking.
5. Press the SYNC button to automatically sync the cook times of both zones.
6. After 15 minutes of cooking, open the drawers and flip the drumsticks to ensure even cooking.
7. Close the drawers and continue cooking until the chicken drumsticks are golden brown and cooked through with an internal temperature of 75°C.
8. Once cooked, remove the chicken drumsticks from the air fryer and let them rest for a few minutes before serving.
9. Serve the **Easy Cajun Chicken Drumsticks** with your favorite side dishes such as roasted vegetables, coleslaw, or a fresh salad.

Chicken Pesto Pizzas

Serves: 4 | Prep & Cook time: 25 Min

- 4 small pizza bases or pita bread
- 4 tablespoons pesto sauce (60ml)
- 2 cooked chicken breasts, shredded
- 100g shredded mozzarella cheese
- 1/2 red onion, thinly sliced
- 1/2 red bell pepper, thinly sliced
- Handful of cherry tomatoes, halved
- Fresh basil leaves, for garnish
- Salt and pepper, to taste.

DIRECTIONS:

1. Place the pizza bases or pita bread on a clean surface.
2. Spread 1 tablespoon of pesto sauce on each pizza base.
3. Divide the shredded chicken evenly among the pizza bases.
4. Sprinkle the shredded mozzarella cheese over the chicken.
5. Arrange the sliced red onion, red bell pepper, and cherry tomatoes on top of the cheese.
6. Season with salt and pepper to taste.
7. In each zone, place two pizzas on the crisper plate. Select the Zone 1, Select AIR FRY function, set the temperature to 200°C, and set the time to 10-12 minutes. Press the MATCH. Press the START/STOP button to begin cooking.
8. After 5 minutes of cooking, open the drawers and rotate the pizzas for even browning.
9. Close the drawers and continue cooking until the pizzas are golden brown and the cheese is melted and bubbly.
10. Once cooked, remove the pizzas from the air fryer and garnish with fresh basil leaves.
11. Serve the **Chicken Pesto Pizzas** hot and enjoy them as a delicious meal. You can customize the toppings according to your preferences, adding ingredients like mushrooms, olives, or fresh herbs.

Ginger Turmeric Chicken Thighs

Serves: 4 | Prep & Cook time: 55 Min

- 8 chicken thighs, bone-in, skin-on
- 2 tablespoons olive oil
- 2 tablespoons soy sauce
- 2 tablespoons honey
- 1 tablespoon grated ginger
- 1 teaspoon ground turmeric
- 1 teaspoon garlic powder
- Salt and pepper, to taste
- Fresh cilantro or parsley, for garnish (optional)

DIRECTIONS:

1. In a bowl, whisk together the olive oil, soy sauce, honey, grated ginger, ground turmeric, garlic powder, salt, and pepper to make the marinade.
2. Place the chicken thighs in a large resealable plastic bag or a bowl. Pour the marinade over the chicken and ensure they are well coated. Let the chicken marinate for at least 15 minutes or up to overnight in the refrigerator for more flavor.
3. Evenly dividing them to cook in two zone. Place the chicken thighs on two crisper plates, skin side down
4. Select Zone 1, Select the AIR FRY function, set the temperature to 180°C, and set the time to 10 minutes. Press MATCH. Press the START/STOP button to begin cooking.
5. After 10 minutes, flip the chicken thighs skin side up. Select the AIR FRY function, set the temperature to 180°C, and set the time to an additional 10-15 minutes, Press the START/STOP button to continue cooking.
6. Once the **chicken thighs** are cooked, remove them from the air fryer and let them rest for a few minutes.
7. Garnish with fresh cilantro or parsley, if desired, before serving.

Lemon Thyme Roasted Chicken

Serves: 5 | Prep & Cook time: 75 Min

- 1 whole chicken (approximately 1.6 kg), giblets removed (or choose a chicken with a weight suitable for 1 zone of your air fryer)
- 2 lemons, divided
- A handful of fresh thyme sprigs
- 4 cloves of garlic, minced
- 2 tablespoons olive oil
- Salt and pepper, to taste

DIRECTIONS:

1. Rinse the chicken inside and out with cold water and pat dry with paper towels.
2. Cut one lemon into slices and stuff them, along with a handful of fresh thyme sprigs, into the cavity of the chicken.
3. In a small bowl, combine the minced garlic, juice of the remaining lemon, olive oil, salt, and pepper to make a marinade.
4. Rub the marinade all over the chicken, ensuring it is evenly coated.
5. In Zone 1, place the chicken on the crisper plate, breast side up. Select the AIR FRY function, set the temperature to 180°C, and set the time to 30 minutes.
6. Press the START/STOP button to begin cooking.
7. After 30 minutes, carefully flip the chicken breast side down. Select the AIR FRY function, set the temperature to 180°C, and set the time to an additional 30 minutes.
8. Press the START/STOP button to resume cooking.
9. Once the cooking time is complete, check the internal temperature of the chicken using a meat thermometer. It should register at least 75°C to ensure it is fully cooked.
10. If needed, cook for additional time until the chicken reaches the desired temperature.
11. Once cooked, remove the chicken from the air fryer and let it rest for a few minutes before carving.
12. Serve the **Lemon Thyme Roasted Chicken** with your choice of side dishes, such as roasted potatoes, steamed vegetables, or a fresh salad.
13. The chicken will be juicy, tender, and infused with the delightful flavors of lemon and thyme.

Spice-Rubbed Chicken Thighs

Serves: 4 | Prep & Cook time: 30 Min

- 8 bone-in, skin-on chicken thighs
- 1 tablespoon paprika
- 1 teaspoon ground cumin
- 1 teaspoon ground coriander
- 1 teaspoon garlic powder
- 1 teaspoon onion powder
- 1/2 teaspoon cayenne pepper (adjust according to spice preference)
- 1 teaspoon salt
- 1/2 teaspoon black pepper
- Cooking spray

DIRECTIONS:

1. In a small bowl, combine the paprika, ground cumin, ground coriander, garlic powder, onion powder, cayenne pepper, salt, and black pepper. Mix well to create the spice rub.
2. Pat dry the chicken thighs with a paper towel and place them on a clean surface.
3. Sprinkle the spice rub evenly over both sides of the chicken thighs, pressing gently to adhere the spices.
4. Insert the crisper plates back into the drawers of the air fryer. Place 4 chicken thighs in each drawer, ensuring they are evenly spaced.
5. In Zone 1, select the AIR FRY function, set the temperature to 200°C, and set the time to 20 minutes. Press the MATCH. Press the START/STOP to begin cooking.
6. After 10 minutes of cooking, open the drawers and lightly spray the chicken thighs with cooking spray to promote browning.
7. Close the drawers and continue cooking for the remaining time.
8. Once the cooking time is complete, remove the chicken thighs from the air fryer and let them rest for a few minutes.
9. Serve the **Spice-Rubbed Chicken Thighs** as desired, such as with a side salad or roasted vegetables.

Pickle Brined Fried Chicken

Serves: 4 | Prep & Cook time: 40 Min

For the Brine:
- 240 ml dill pickle juice
- 240 ml buttermilk
- 4 bone-in, skin-on chicken pieces (such as drumsticks or thighs)

For the Coating:
- 120 grams all-purpose flour
- 1 teaspoon paprika
- 1 teaspoon garlic powder
- 1 teaspoon onion powder
- 1/2 teaspoon salt
- 1/4 teaspoon black pepper
- Cooking spray

DIRECTIONS:

1. In a large bowl, combine the dill pickle juice and buttermilk to create the brine.
2. Add the chicken pieces to the brine, making sure they are fully submerged. Cover the bowl and refrigerate for 1-2 hours to allow the chicken to brine.
3. In a shallow dish, combine the all-purpose flour, paprika, garlic powder, onion powder, salt, and black pepper. Mix well.
4. Remove each chicken piece from the brine, allowing any excess liquid to drip off, and coat it in the flour mixture, pressing gently to ensure the coating adheres.
5. Insert the crisper plate back into the drawers of the air fryer. Place 4 chicken pieces in Zone 1. Select the AIR FRY, set temperature to 200°C in 20 minutes. Press the START/STOP.
6. After 15 minutes of cooking, open the drawer and lightly spray the chicken pieces with cooking spray to promote browning.
7. Close the drawer and continue cooking for the remaining time.
8. Once the cooking time is complete, remove the chicken pieces from the air fryer and let them rest for a few minutes.
9. Serve the **Pickle Brined Fried Chicken** hot with your choice of sides and dipping sauces.

Teriyaki Chicken Legs

Serves: 2 | Prep & Cook time: 50 Min

- 4 chicken legs
- 4 tablespoons soy sauce
- 2 tablespoons honey
- 1 tablespoon rice vinegar
- 1 tablespoon minced garlic
- 1 tablespoon grated ginger
- 1 tablespoon sesame oil
- 1 tablespoon cornstarch
- 2 tablespoons water
- Sesame seeds, for garnish
- Chopped spring onions, for garnish.

DIRECTIONS:

1. In a bowl, mix together the soy sauce, honey, rice vinegar, minced garlic, grated ginger, and sesame oil to make the teriyaki sauce.
2. Place the chicken legs in a shallow dish and pour the teriyaki sauce over them, ensuring they are well coated. Let them marinate for about 10 minutes.
3. In Zone 1, place the chicken legs on the crisper plate. Select the AIR FRY function, set the temperature to 180°C, and set the time to 25-30 minutes. Press the START/STOP button to begin cooking.
4. After 15 minutes of cooking, open the drawers and flip the chicken legs to ensure even cooking.
5. In a small bowl, mix the cornstarch and water to create a slurry. Brush the slurry over the chicken legs to create a glaze.
6. Close the drawers and continue cooking until the chicken legs are cooked through and the skin is crispy.
7. Once cooked, remove the chicken legs from the air fryer and sprinkle with sesame seeds and chopped spring onions for garnish.
8. Serve the **Teriyaki Chicken Legs** hot with steamed rice or noodles and your choice of vegetables for a complete meal.

French Garlic Chicken

Serves: 4 | Prep & Cook time: 45 Min

- 4 bone-in, skin-on chicken thighs
- 4 garlic cloves, minced
- 2 tablespoons butter, melted
- 2 tablespoons olive oil
- 2 tablespoons fresh lemon juice
- 1 teaspoon dried thyme
- 1 teaspoon dried rosemary
- Salt and pepper, to taste
- Fresh parsley, chopped for garnish.

DIRECTIONS:

1. In a small bowl, mix together the minced garlic, melted butter, olive oil, lemon juice, dried thyme, dried rosemary, salt, and pepper to make a marinade.
2. Place the chicken thighs in a shallow dish and pour the marinade over them, ensuring they are well coated. Let them marinate for about 10 minutes.
3. In Zone 1, place the chicken thighs on the crisper plate. Select the AIR FRY function, set the temperature to 180°C, and set the time to 25-30 minutes. Press the START/STOP button to begin cooking.
4. After 15 minutes of cooking, open the drawers and flip the chicken thighs to ensure even cooking. Continue cooking until the chicken thighs are cooked through and the skin is crispy.
5. Once cooked, remove the chicken thighs from the air fryer and garnish with fresh chopped parsley.
6. Serve the **French Garlic Chicken** hot with your choice of side dishes such as roasted potatoes, steamed vegetables, or a fresh salad.

Cheese-Encrusted Chicken Tenderloins with Peanuts

Serves: 4 | Prep & Cook time: 30 Min

- 500g chicken tenderloins
- 100g grated Parmesan cheese
- 100g breadcrumbs
- 50g roasted peanuts, crushed
- 2 eggs, beaten
- 2 tablespoons olive oil
- 1 teaspoon dried thyme
- 1/2 teaspoon garlic powder
- Salt and pepper, to taste

DIRECTIONS:

1. In a shallow bowl, combine the grated Parmesan cheese, breadcrumbs, crushed peanuts, dried thyme, garlic powder, salt, and pepper. Mix well.
2. Dip each chicken tenderloin into the beaten eggs, allowing any excess to drip off.
3. Coat the egg-coated chicken tenderloin with the cheese, breadcrumb, and peanut mixture, pressing gently to adhere the coating to the chicken.
4. Repeat the process with the remaining chicken tenderloins.
5. In Zone 1, place the coated chicken tenderloins on the crisper plate. Select the AIR FRY function, set the temperature to 200°C, and set time to 15 minutes. Press the START/STOP button to begin cooking.
6. While the chicken tenderloins are cooking, prepare any desired sauce or dip to accompany the dish.
7. After the cooking time is complete, remove the chicken tenderloins from the air fryer and let them cool for a few minutes before serving.
8. Enjoy the **Cheese-Encrusted Chicken Tenderloins with Peanuts** as a flavorful and crispy dish.

Bacon-Wrapped Chicken Breasts Rolls

Serves: 4 | Prep & Cook time: 35 Min

- 4 boneless, skinless chicken breasts
- 8 slices of streaky bacon
- 100g cream cheese
- 1 teaspoon garlic powder
- 1 teaspoon dried thyme
- Salt and pepper, to taste
- Toothpicks (for securing)

DIRECTIONS:

1. Pound the chicken breasts to flatten them slightly, making them easier to roll.
2. In a small bowl, mix the cream cheese, garlic powder, dried thyme, salt, and pepper.
3. Spread a spoonful of the cream cheese mixture onto each chicken breast.
4. Roll up each chicken breast tightly, starting from one end.
5. Wrap two slices of streaky bacon around each rolled chicken breast, securing them with toothpicks.
6. In Zone 1, place the bacon-wrapped chicken breast rolls on the crisper plate. Select the AIR FRY function, set the temperature to 200°C, and set the time to 18-20 minutes. Press the START/STOP.
7. After the cooking time is complete, remove the bacon-wrapped chicken breast rolls from the air fryer and let them cool for a few minutes.
8. Carefully remove the toothpicks before serving.
9. Enjoy the **Bacon-Wrapped Chicken Breast Rolls** as a delicious and satisfying dish. Serve them with your favorite sides, such as roasted vegetables or a fresh salad, for a complete meal.

Chicken & Broccoli Casserole

Serves: 4 | Prep & Cook time: 35 Min

- 2 boneless, skinless chicken breasts, cooked and shredded
- 200g broccoli florets, steamed
- 100g grated cheddar cheese
- 120ml sour cream
- 120ml mayonnaise
- 25g grated Parmesan cheese
- 2 cloves garlic, minced
- 1/2 teaspoon dried thyme
- 1/2 teaspoon dried oregano
- 1/2 teaspoon salt
- 1/4 teaspoon black pepper.

DIRECTIONS:

1. In a large mixing bowl, combine the shredded chicken, steamed broccoli florets, grated cheddar cheese, sour cream, mayonnaise, grated Parmesan cheese, minced garlic, dried thyme, dried oregano, salt, and black pepper. Mix well until all the ingredients are evenly combined.
2. Transfer the chicken and broccoli mixture into a greased baking dish that fits into the Zone 1.
3. Place the baking dish into Zone 1 of the air fryer. Select the AIR FRY function, set the temperature to 180°C, and set the cooking time to 20 minutes.
4. Once cooking time is complete, check if the casserole is fully heated through and the cheese is melted and bubbly? Cook for an additional 5 minutes, if need.
5. Carefully remove the **Chicken and Broccoli Casserole** from the air fryer and let it cool for a few minutes before serving.

Chicken with Masala Fries

Serves: 2 | Prep & Cook time: 40 Min

- 2 chicken breasts, boneless and skinless
- 2 tablespoons plain yogurt
- 1 tablespoon lemon juice
- 2 teaspoons ginger-garlic paste
- 1 teaspoon ground cumin
- 1 teaspoon ground coriander
- 1/2 teaspoon turmeric powder
- 1/2 teaspoon paprika
- 1/2 teaspoon garam masala
- Salt to taste
- 2 large potatoes, cut into fries
- 2 tablespoons olive oil
- 1 teaspoon chili powder
- 1/2 teaspoon chaat masala
- Fresh coriander leaves, for garnish
- Lemon wedges, for serving.

DIRECTIONS:

1. In a bowl, combine the yogurt, lemon juice, ginger-garlic paste, cumin, coriander, turmeric, paprika, garam masala, and salt. Mix well to make a marinade.
2. Add the chicken breasts to the marinade and coat them thoroughly. Allow the chicken to marinate for at least 30 minutes, or refrigerate overnight for enhanced flavor.
3. In a separate bowl, toss the potato fries with olive oil, chili powder, and salt until well coated.
4. Place the marinated chicken breasts in Zone 1 of the air fryer, Select the AIR FRY function, set the temperature to 200°C, and set the time to 12-15 minutes. Press the START/STOP, flipping halfway through, or until the chicken is cooked through and golden brown.
5. While the chicken is cooking, place the seasoned potato fries in Zone 2 of the air fryer basket. AIR FRY for 20-25 minutes in 180°C, shaking the basket occasionally, or until the fries are crispy and golden.
6. Once cooked, remove the chicken and fries from the air fryer and sprinkle the fries with chaat masala for extra flavor.
7. Serve the **chicken with masala fries** on a platter. Garnish with fresh coriander leaves and serve with lemon wedges on the side.

Chicken Fajitas & Spicy Roast Potatoes

Serves: 4 | Prep & Cook time: 35 Min

FAJITAS:

- 3 chicken breasts
- 1 tablespoon smoked paprika
- 1 tablespoon ground coriander
- 1 teaspoon ground cumin
- 1 teaspoon garlic powder 1/2 teaspoon dried chilli flakes
- 1 teaspoon dried oregano
- 4 tablespoons olive oil
- Juice of 1 lime
- Salt and freshly ground
- black pepper
- 1 onion, sliced
- 1 red pepper, sliced
- 1 yellow pepper, sliced
- 8 medium tortillas

SPICY POTATOES:

- 1kg baby potatoes,
- cut in quarters
- 3 tablespoons olive oil
- 2 teaspoons hot paprika
- 1 tablespoon garlic powder
- 1 tablespoon smoked paprika
- 1 teaspoon sea salt.

DIRECTIONS

1. Slice chicken breasts into thin strips.
2. Add spices, herbs, oil and lime juice into a large bowl, season to taste and mix together.
3. Stir in chicken pieces, onion and peppers, mix all together until everything is coated in the marinade.
4. In another bowl, toss potatoes in oil and spices.
5. Insert a crisper plate in both drawers. Add chicken and vegetables to Zone 1 drawer and potatoes to Zone 2 drawer and insert into unit.
6. Select Zone 1, select AIR FRY, set temperature to 200°C and set time to 20 minutes. Select Zone 2, select ROAST, set temperature to 180°C and set time to 25 minutes. Select SYNC. Press the START/STOP button to begin cooking.
7. After 10 minutes, give both drawers a shake or stir. Repeat again after 15 minutes.
8. When Zone 1 time reaches 0, check chicken is cooked. Cooking is complete when the internal temperature reaches at least 75°C on an instant read thermometer.
9. Serve chicken and vegetables wrapped in the tortillas with the potatoes on the side.

Bruschetta Chicken

Serves: 4 | Prep & Cook time: 35 Min

- 4 boneless, skinless chicken breasts
- 2 tablespoons olive oil
- 2 cloves garlic, minced
- 1 teaspoon dried basil
- 1 teaspoon dried oregano
- Salt and pepper to taste
- 4 slices mozzarella cheese
- 4 large tomato slices
- Fresh basil leaves, for garnish

For the Bruschetta Topping:

- 2 large tomatoes, diced
- 2 cloves garlic, minced
- 2 tablespoons extra-virgin olive oil
- 1 tablespoon balsamic vinegar
- 1 tablespoon fresh basil, chopped
- Salt and pepper to taste

DIRECTIONS

1. In a bowl, combine the diced tomatoes, minced garlic, olive oil, balsamic vinegar, fresh basil, salt, and pepper. Mix well to make the bruschetta topping. Set aside.
2. Place the chicken breasts on a clean surface and drizzle them with olive oil. Rub the minced garlic, dried basil, dried oregano, salt, and pepper onto both sides of the chicken.
3. Insert the crisper plates back into the drawers of the air fryer. Place 2 chicken breasts in each drawer, ensuring they are evenly spaced.
4. In Zone 1, select the AIR FRY function, set the temperature to 200°C, and set the time to 15 minutes. Press the MATCH. Press the START/STOP to begin cooking.
5. While the chicken cooks, prepare the tomato slices and mozzarella cheese.
6. After 10 minutes of cooking, open the drawers and place a slice of mozzarella cheese on each chicken breast. Close the drawers and continue cooking.
7. Once the cooking time is complete, remove the chicken from the air fryer and let it rest for a few minutes.
8. Meanwhile, lightly toast the slices of bread by place them on the crisper plates in 1 zone, select ROAST, temperature to 180°C and the time to 2 minutes.
9. Place a tomato slice on top of each chicken breast, followed by a spoonful of the bruschetta topping.
10. Garnish with fresh basil leaves and serve the **Bruschetta Chicken** with toasted bread slices.

Golden Chicken Cutlets

Serves: 4 | Prep & Cook time: 25 Min

- 4 boneless, skinless chicken breasts
- 240g breadcrumbs
- 2 teaspoons paprika
- 1 teaspoon garlic powder
- 1 teaspoon dried thyme
- 1 teaspoon dried parsley
- Salt and pepper to taste
- 2 large eggs
- Cooking spray

For the Lemon-Herb Sauce:

- 120g mayonnaise
- 1 tablespoon lemon juice
- 1 teaspoon Dijon mustard
- 1 tablespoon fresh parsley, chopped
- 1 tablespoon fresh dill, chopped
- Salt and pepper to taste

DIRECTIONS

1. In a shallow dish, combine the breadcrumbs, paprika, garlic powder, dried thyme, dried parsley, salt, and pepper. Mix well.
2. In another shallow dish, whisk the eggs until well beaten.
3. Dip each chicken breast into the beaten eggs, allowing any excess to drip off, then coat it with the breadcrumb mixture. Press the breadcrumbs onto the chicken to ensure they adhere well.
4. Insert the crisper plates back into the drawers of the air fryer. Place 2 chicken breasts in each drawer, ensuring they are evenly spaced.
5. In Zone 1, select the AIR FRY function, set the temperature to 200°C, and set the time to 10 minutes.
6. Press the MATCH. Press the START/STOP button to begin cooking.
7. After 6 minutes of cooking, open the drawers and lightly spray the chicken cutlets with cooking spray to promote browning.
8. Close the drawers and continue cooking for the remaining time.
9. While the chicken cooks, prepare the lemon-herb sauce. In a bowl, combine the mayonnaise, lemon juice, Dijon mustard, fresh parsley, fresh dill, salt, and pepper. Mix well.
10. Once the cooking time is complete, remove the chicken cutlets from the air fryer and let them rest for a few minutes.
11. Serve the **Golden Chicken Cutlets** with the lemon-herb sauce on the side.

Chicken Croquettes with Creole Sauce

Serves: 4 | Prep & Cook time: 40 Min

INGREDIENTS

For the Chicken Croquettes:

- 500g cooked chicken breast, finely shredded
- 1 small onion, finely chopped
- 2 cloves of garlic, minced
- 2 tablespoons fresh parsley, chopped
- 1 teaspoon dried thyme
- 1 teaspoon paprika
- 1/2 teaspoon salt
- 1/4 teaspoon black pepper
- 2 eggs, beaten
- 50g breadcrumbs
- 50g all-purpose flour
- Cooking spray

For the Creole Sauce:

- 2 tablespoons butter
- 1 small onion, finely chopped
- 1 small green bell pepper, finely chopped
- 2 cloves of garlic, minced
- 1 can (400g) diced tomatoes
- 1 teaspoon paprika
- 1/2 teaspoon dried oregano
- 1/4 teaspoon cayenne pepper (adjust according to your spice preference)
- Salt and pepper, to taste.

DIRECTIONS

1. In a mixing bowl, combine the shredded chicken, chopped onion, minced garlic, fresh parsley, dried thyme, paprika, salt, and black pepper. Mix well.
2. Shape the chicken mixture into small croquettes.
3. Place the beaten eggs, flour, and breadcrumbs in separate bowls for coating.
4. Dip each chicken croquette in the flour, then the beaten eggs, and finally coat with breadcrumbs.
5. Evenly dividing them (to cook in both zone) and place the chicken croquettes on the crisper plates.
6. In Zone 1, Select the AIR FRY function, set the temperature to 180°C, and set the time to 20 minutes. Press the MATCH. Press the START/STOP button to begin cooking.
7. In the meantime, prepare the Creole sauce. In a saucepan, melt the butter over medium heat. Add the chopped onion, green bell pepper, and minced garlic. Sauté until softened.
8. Add the diced tomatoes, paprika, dried oregano, cayenne pepper, salt, and pepper to the saucepan. Stir well and let it simmer for about 10 minutes, until the flavors meld together.
9. After 10 minutes of cooking the chicken croquettes, open the drawers and flip them to ensure even cooking. Spray them with cooking spray for a crispier texture.
10. Close the drawers and continue cooking until the chicken croquettes are golden brown and cooked through.
11. Once cooked, remove the chicken croquettes from the air fryer and serve them hot with the prepared Creole sauce on the side.
12. Enjoy the **Chicken Croquettes with Creole Sauce** as a delicious appetizer or main course.

Stuffed Turkey Roulade

Serves: 4 | Prep & Cook time: 55 Min

- 500 grams boneless turkey breast
- 100 grams fresh spinach leaves
- 50 grams feta cheese, crumbled
- 50 grams sun-dried tomatoes, chopped
- 25 grams pine nuts
- 1 tablespoon olive oil
- 1 teaspoon dried oregano
- 1/2 teaspoon garlic powder
- Salt and pepper, to taste

DIRECTIONS

1. Lay the boneless turkey breast flat on a cutting board and carefully butterfly it by making a horizontal cut through the center, taking care not to cut all the way through. Open up the turkey breast like a book.
2. In Zone 1, lay down a sheet of plastic wrap on the crisper plate. Place the butterflied turkey breast on the plastic wrap and cover it with another sheet of plastic wrap.
3. Use a meat mallet or rolling pin to flatten the turkey breast to an even thickness.
4. Remove the top sheet of plastic wrap. Season the turkey breast with dried oregano, garlic powder, salt, and pepper.
5. In Zone 2, heat the olive oil. Add the fresh spinach leaves, select the AIR FRY function, set the temperature to 180°C, and set the time to 4-5 minutes. Press the START/STOP.
6. Spread the wilted spinach evenly over the turkey breast.
7. Sprinkle the crumbled feta cheese, chopped sun-dried tomatoes, and pine nuts over the spinach layer.
8. Starting from one end, carefully roll up the turkey breast tightly, using the plastic wrap to help you.
9. Remove the plastic wrap from the rolled turkey roulade.
10. In Zone 1, select the AIR FRY function, set the temperature to 180°C, and set the time to 30-35 minutes. Press the START/STOP.
11. Once the cooking time is complete, remove the drawers from the air fryer and let the turkey roulade rest for a few minutes before slicing.
12. Slice the Stuffed Turkey Roulade into portions and serve hot.
13. Enjoy the flavorful **Stuffed Turkey Roulade** with your choice of sides, such as roasted vegetables and mashed potatoes.

Chicken, Courgette, & Spinach Salad

Serves: 4 | Prep & Cook time: 30 Min

For the Chicken:

- 4 boneless, skinless chicken breasts
- 1 tablespoon olive oil
- 1 teaspoon paprika
- 1/2 teaspoon garlic powder
- 1/2 teaspoon onion powder
- 1/2 teaspoon dried thyme
- Salt and pepper to taste

For the Salad:

- 2 medium courgettes (zucchini), thinly sliced
- 200 grams baby spinach leaves
- 200 grams cherry tomatoes, halved
- 1/2 red onion, thinly sliced
- 50 grams feta cheese, crumbled

For the Dressing:

- 3 tablespoons extra virgin olive oil
- 2 tablespoons lemon juice
- 1 teaspoon Dijon mustard
- 1 teaspoon honey
- Salt and pepper to taste

DIRECTIONS

1. In a small bowl, combine the paprika, garlic powder, onion powder, dried thyme, salt, and pepper to create the seasoning for the chicken.
2. Rub the chicken breasts with olive oil and then sprinkle the seasoning mixture evenly on both sides of each chicken breast.
3. Place the seasoned chicken breasts in Zone 1 of the air fryer.
4. In Zone 2, place the thinly sliced courgettes (zucchini) on the crisper plate.
5. In Zone 1, select the AIR FRY function, set the temperature to 200°C, and set the time to 15 minutes.
6. In Zone 2, select the AIR FRY function, set the temperature to 180°C, and set the time to 7 minutes.
7. (If like, Press the SYNC button to automatically sync the cook times of both zones). Press the START/STOP button to begin cooking.
8. After haft of cooking time, open the drawer in each zone and gently shake it.
9. While the chicken and courgettes are cooking, prepare the salad by combining the baby spinach leaves, cherry tomatoes, red onion, and crumbled feta cheese in a large bowl.
10. In a separate small bowl, whisk together the extra virgin olive oil, lemon juice, Dijon mustard, honey, salt, and pepper to create the dressing.
11. Once the cooking time is complete, remove the chicken breasts and courgettes from the air fryer.
12. Allow the chicken to rest for a few minutes, then slice it into thin strips.
13. Add the cooked courgettes and sliced chicken to the salad bowl.
14. Drizzle the dressing over the salad and toss well to coat all the ingredients.
15. Serve the **Chicken, Courgette, and Spinach Salad** immediately as a delicious and healthy meal.

Barbecued Chicken with Creamy Coleslaw

Serves: 4 | Prep & Cook time: 40 Min

For the Barbecued Chicken:

- 2 chicken breasts
- 4 tablespoons barbecue sauce
- 1 tablespoon olive oil
- 1 teaspoon smoked paprika
- 1/2 teaspoon garlic powder
- Salt and pepper, to taste

For the Creamy Coleslaw:

- 200 grams shredded cabbage
- 50 grams grated carrot
- 2 tablespoons mayonnaise
- 1 tablespoon Greek yogurt
- 1 tablespoon apple cider vinegar
- 1 teaspoon Dijon mustard
- 1 teaspoon honey
- Salt and pepper, to taste

DIRECTIONS

For the Barbecued Chicken:

1. In a bowl, combine the barbecue sauce, olive oil, smoked paprika, garlic powder, salt, and pepper. Mix well.
2. Place the chicken breasts in a shallow dish and pour half of the barbecue sauce mixture over them, reserving the remaining sauce for basting.
3. In Zone 1, place the chicken breasts on the crisper plate. Select the AIR FRY function, set the temperature to 180°C, and set the time to 20-25 minutes. Press the START/STOP button to begin cooking.
4. After 10 minutes of cooking, open the drawers and brush the chicken breasts with the reserved barbecue sauce mixture.
5. Close the drawer and continue cooking until the chicken is cooked through.
6. Once cooked, remove the chicken from the air fryer and let it rest for a few minutes before slicing.

For the Creamy Coleslaw:

1. In a large bowl, combine the shredded cabbage and grated carrot.
2. In a separate small bowl, whisk together the mayonnaise, Greek yogurt, apple cider vinegar, Dijon mustard, honey, salt, and pepper until well combined.
3. Pour the dressing over the cabbage and carrot mixture. Toss until the vegetables are well coated.
4. Adjust the seasoning according to your taste preferences.
5. Serve the barbecued chicken alongside the creamy coleslaw. It pairs well with additional barbecue sauce or a side of fries

Chorizo & Beef Burger

Serves: 4 | Prep & Cook time: 30 Min

- 300g beef mince
- 100g chorizo, finely chopped
- 1 small onion, finely chopped
- 2 cloves of garlic, minced
- 1 teaspoon smoked paprika
- 1 teaspoon dried oregano
- Salt and pepper, to taste
- 4 burger buns
- Lettuce leaves
- Tomato slices
- Red onion slices
- Cheese slices (optional)
- Condiments of your choice (such as ketchup, mayonnaise, or mustard)

DIRECTIONS:

1. In a bowl, combine the beef mince, chopped chorizo, onion, garlic, smoked paprika, dried oregano, salt, and pepper. Mix well to combine all the ingredients.
2. Divide the mixture into four equal portions and shape them into burger patties.
3. Place the burger patties in Zone 1 of the air fryer. Select Zone 1, then select the AIR FRY function. Set the temperature to 200°C and the time to 15 minutes. Press the START/STOP button to begin cooking. Flipping halfway through, until the burgers are cooked through and nicely browned.
4. While the burgers are cooking, you can lightly toast the burger buns if desired.
5. Assemble the burgers by placing lettuce leaves, tomato slices, and red onion slices on the bottom half of each burger bun. If using cheese, place a cheese slice on top of the burger patty.
6. Once the burgers are cooked, place them on the prepared burger buns. Add your desired condiments on top.
7. Serve the **Chorizo and Beef Burgers** immediately with your favorite side dishes.

Chapter 5: Beef, Pork, & Lamb

Italian Sausage & Cheese Meatballs

Serves: 4 | Prep & Cook time: 30 Min

- 500g Italian sausage meat
- 50g breadcrumbs
- 25g grated Parmesan cheese
- 25g finely chopped parsley
- 1/2 teaspoon garlic powder
- 1/2 teaspoon dried oregano
- 1/4 teaspoon salt
- 1/4 teaspoon black pepper
- 25g grated mozzarella cheese
- Marinara sauce, for serving

DIRECTIONS:

1. In a large mixing bowl, combine the Italian sausage meat, breadcrumbs, grated Parmesan cheese, chopped parsley, garlic powder, dried oregano, salt, and black pepper. Mix well until all ingredients are evenly incorporated.
2. Take a small portion of the meat mixture and flatten it in the palm of your hand. Place a small amount (about 1/4 teaspoon) of grated mozzarella cheese in the center. Fold the meat mixture around the cheese, shaping it into a ball. Repeat this process with the remaining meat mixture and cheese.
3. Once the air fryer has preheated, place the meatballs in Zone 1 of the air fryer. Select Zone 1, then select the AIR FRY function. Set the temperature to 180°C and the time to 15 minutes. Press the START/STOP button to begin cooking.
4. Cook the meatballs until they are golden brown and cooked through, with an internal temperature of 75°C. You can check the doneness by cutting one meatball open to ensure it's fully cooked.
5. Once cooked, remove the meatballs from the air fryer and let them cool slightly. Serve the **meatballs with marinara sauce** for dipping or as a topping.

Fried Pork & Sweet Potato Fries

Serves: 4 | Prep & Cook time: 40 Min

- 240g plain flour
- 2 large eggs
- 1 teaspoon smoked paprika
- 1 teaspoon garlic powder
- 1 teaspoon sea salt
- 1 teaspoon ground black pepper
- 1/2 teaspoon chilli powder
- 2-4 boneless pork chops, cut in half lengthwise, pounded 1cm thick
- 500g frozen sweet potato fries.

DIRECTIONS:

1. Place flour, paprika, garlic powder, salt, pepper and chilli powder in a shallow bowl and mix well.
2. Place eggs in a shallow bowl and whisk thoroughly.
3. Working one at a time, dip the pork chops in egg, then in seasoned flour, then again in egg, then again in flour. Set aside.
4. Insert crisper plates in both drawers. Add pork chops to Zone 1 drawer and fries to Zone 2 drawer. Insert both drawers into unit.
5. Select Zone 1, select ROAST, set temperature to 200°C and set time to 15 minutes. Select Zone 2, select AIR FRY, set temperature to 180°C and set time to 24 minutes. Select SYNC. Press the START/STOP button to begin cooking.
6. After 10 minutes, remove Zone 2 drawer and shake drawer for 10 seconds. Reinsert drawer to continue cooking. Repeat after 15 and 20 minutes.
7. After 8 minutes, remove Zone 2 drawer and flip pork chops using silicone-tipped tongs.
8. When cooking is complete, serve **pork chops with fries**.

Bacon Wrapped Pork Chops & Quinoa

Serves: 4 | Prep & Cook time: 45 Min

- 4 boneless pork chops(125g-175g each)
- 4 teaspoons sea salt
- 4 teaspoons ground black pepper
- 8 rashers uncooked bacon
- 180g quinoa
- 375ml chicken stock
- 1 clove garlic, peeled, minced
- 1 bunch spring onions, slice.

DIRECTIONS:

1. Season all sides of the pork chops with salt and pepper, then wrap each one with two strips of bacon.
2. Install a crisping plate in the Zone 1 basket, then place chops in the basket and insert basket in unit.
3. With no crisping plate installed, place quinoa, stock, garlic, and spring onions in the Zone 2 basket and stir to combine.
4. Select Zone 1, select AIR FRY, set temperature to 200°C, and set time to 25 minutes. Select Zone 2, select BAKE, set temperature to 200°C and set time for 35 minutes. Select SYNC. Press the START/ PAUSE button to begin cooking.
5. When the Zone 1 time reaches 10 minutes, remove basket from unit and flip chops using silicone-tipped tongs. Reinsert basket to continue cooking.
6. When cooking is complete, serve **pork chops with quinoa**.

Cajun Bacon Pork Loin Fillet

Serves: 6 | Prep & Cook time: 40 Min

- 1.2 kg pork loin fillet
- 8 slices bacon
- 2 tablespoons Cajun seasoning
- 2 tablespoons olive oil
- Salt and pepper, to taste.

DIRECTIONS:

1. Season the pork loin fillet with Cajun seasoning, salt, and pepper, ensuring it is evenly coated.
2. Wrap the seasoned pork loin fillet with bacon slices, securing them with toothpicks if necessary.
3. Drizzle olive oil over the bacon-wrapped pork loin fillet.
4. Place the pork loin fillet in both zone of the air fryer. Select Zone 1, choose the AIR FRY program, set the temperature to 200°C, and set the time to 25 minutes. Select MATCH to duplicate settings across both zones. Press the START/STOP button to begin cooking.
5. After 12 minutes of cooking, open the air fryer and carefully flip the pork loin fillet to ensure even browning.
6. Close the air fryer and continue cooking for the remaining time or until the internal temperature of the pork reaches 63°C. Adjust the cooking time as needed based on the thickness of the fillet.
7. Once cooked, remove the **Cajun Bacon Pork Loin Fillet** from the air fryer and let it rest for a few minutes before slicing.
8. Slice the pork loin fillet into thick slices and serve hot.

Lemon Pork with Marjoram

Serves: 4 | Prep & Cook time: 35 Min

- 600g pork tenderloin, sliced into medallions
- 2 tablespoons olive oil
- 2 cloves garlic, minced
- 1 tablespoon fresh marjoram leaves, chopped
- Juice of 1 lemon
- Zest of 1 lemon
- Salt and pepper, to taste.

DIRECTIONS:

1. In a bowl, combine the lemon zest, lemon juice, olive oil, minced garlic, chopped marjoram, salt, and pepper. Mix well to create a marinade.
2. Add the pork medallions to the marinade and toss to coat them evenly. Let them marinate for at least 10 minutes.
3. Place the marinated pork medallions in Zone 1 of the air fryer. Select Zone 1, choose the AIR FRY program, set the temperature to 200°C, and set the time to 20 minutes. Press the START/STOP button to begin cooking.
4. After 10 minutes of cooking, open the air fryer and carefully flip the pork medallions to ensure even cooking.
5. Close the air fryer and continue cooking for the remaining time or until the pork is cooked through and golden brown.
6. Once cooked, remove the Lemon Pork with Marjoram from the air fryer and let it rest for a few minutes before serving.
7. Serve the pork medallions with your choice of sides, such as roasted vegetables or a fresh salad.
8. Enjoy the zesty and flavorful **Lemon Pork with Marjoram** prepared in the Ninja Dual Zone air fryer. The combination of lemon, garlic, and marjoram adds a delicious twist to the pork medallions, making it a tasty and satisfying dish for any occasion.

Reuben Beef Rolls with Thousand Island Sauce

Serves: 10 rolls | Prep & Cook time: 40 Min

- 500g thinly sliced roast beef
- 200g sauerkraut
- 10 slices Swiss cheese
- 10 slices rye bread
- 120ml Thousand Island dressing
- Butter, for brushing.

DIRECTIONS:

1. Lay out the rye bread slices and brush one side of each slice with butter.
2. On each bread slice, layer a slice of Swiss cheese, a portion of roast beef, a spoonful of sauerkraut, and a drizzle of Thousand Island dressing.
3. Roll up the bread slices tightly and secure with toothpicks.
4. Place the beef rolls in both zone of the air fryer basket.
5. Select Zone 1, choose the AIR FRY function, set the temperature to 200°C, and the time to 15 minutes. Select MATCH. Press the START/STOP.
6. While the beef rolls are cooking, prepare the dipping sauce by combining the remaining Thousand Island dressing with any desired additional seasonings.
7. After 15 minutes, carefully remove the beef rolls from the air fryer and let them cool slightly.
8. Serve the **Reuben beef rolls with the Thousand Island dipping sauce**.

For Thousand Island Sauce:

- 120 ml mayonnaise
- 30 ml ketchup
- 15 ml sweet pickle relish
- 15 ml finely chopped onion
- 5 ml white vinegar
- 5 ml Worcestershire sauce
- Salt and pepper to taste.

Directions:
- In a bowl, combine the mayonnaise, ketchup, sweet pickle relish, chopped onion, white vinegar, and Worcestershire sauce.
- Mix well until all the ingredients are thoroughly combined. Season with salt and pepper to taste.
- Once prepared, refrigerate the Thousand Island sauce for at least 30 minutes to allow the flavors to meld together.

Beef & Spinach Rolls

Serves: 2 | Prep & Cook time: 30 Min

- 4 thin beef slices (such as sirloin or minute steaks)
- 60 g fresh spinach leaves
- 1/2 onion, thinly sliced
- 2 cloves garlic, minced
- 1 tablespoon olive oil
- Salt and pepper, to taste
- 1/2 teaspoon dried thyme
- Toothpicks.

DIRECTIONS:

1. In a skillet, heat olive oil over medium heat. Add the minced garlic and sliced onion. Sauté until the onion becomes translucent and the garlic is fragrant.
2. Add the fresh spinach leaves to the skillet and cook until wilted. Season with salt, pepper, and dried thyme. Remove from heat and let the mixture cool slightly.
3. Lay out the beef slices on a clean surface. Divide the spinach and onion mixture equally among the beef slices, spreading it evenly.
4. Roll up each beef slice tightly and secure with toothpicks to hold the rolls together.
5. Place the beef rolls in Zone 1. Select Zone 1, then select the AIR FRY function. Set the temperature to 200°C and the time to 12-15 minutes. Press the START/STOP button to begin cooking.
6. Flip the beef rolls halfway through the cooking time to ensure even browning.
7. Once the beef rolls are cooked and golden brown, remove them from the air fryer and let them cool slightly.
8. Serve the **beef and spinach rolls** as a delicious appetizer or main dish. Remove the toothpicks before serving.

Pork Medallions with Endive Salad

Serves: 4 | Prep & Cook time: 35 Min

- 500g pork tenderloin, cut into medallions
- 2 tablespoons olive oil
- 2 cloves garlic, minced
- 1 teaspoon dried thyme
- Salt and pepper, to taste
- 2 endives, thinly sliced
- 1 small red onion, thinly sliced
- 100g cherry tomatoes, halved
- 50g feta cheese, crumbled
- 2 tablespoons lemon juice
- 2 tablespoons extra virgin olive oil.

DIRECTIONS:

1. In a bowl, combine the minced garlic, dried thyme, salt, pepper, and 1 tablespoon of olive oil. Mix well.
2. Place the pork medallions in a separate bowl and coat them with the garlic and thyme mixture.
3. Place the seasoned pork medallions in Zone 1 of the air fryer. Select Zone 1, choose the AIR FRY program, set the temperature to 200°C, and set the time to 10 minutes. Press the START/STOP button to begin cooking.
4. While the pork is cooking, prepare the endive salad. In a large bowl, combine the sliced endives, red onion, cherry tomatoes, and crumbled feta cheese.
5. In a small bowl, whisk together the lemon juice, extra virgin olive oil, salt, and pepper. Pour the dressing over the salad and toss to combine.
6. After 10 minutes of cooking, carefully flip the pork medallions using tongs and cook for another 5-8 minutes or until they reach an internal temperature of 63°C.
7. Remove the pork medallions from the air fryer and let them rest for a few minutes before serving.
8. Serve the **pork medallions alongside the refreshing endive salad**.

Cheese Crusted Pork Chops

Serves: 5 | Prep & Cook time: 35 Min

- 5 pork chops
- 120g breadcrumbs
- 120g grated cheddar cheese
- 1 teaspoon dried thyme
- 1 teaspoon paprika
- Salt and pepper, to taste
- 2 eggs, beaten
- Cooking spray

DIRECTIONS:

1. Preheat Zone 1 of the Ninja Dual Zone air fryer to 200°C for 5 minutes.
2. In a shallow bowl, combine the breadcrumbs, grated cheddar cheese, dried thyme, paprika, salt, and pepper. Mix well.
3. Dip each pork chop into the beaten eggs, making sure to coat both sides.
4. Press each pork chop into the breadcrumb and cheese mixture, ensuring a thick and even coating on both sides. Place the coated pork chops on a plate.
5. Spray Zone 1 of the air fryer with cooking spray to prevent sticking.
6. Place the cheese-crusted pork chops in Zone 1 of the air fryer. Select Zone 1, choose the AIR FRY program, set the temperature to 200°C, and set the time to 15 minutes. Press the START/STOP button to begin cooking.
7. After 15 minutes of cooking, carefully flip the pork chops using tongs and cook for another 5 minutes or until they reach an internal temperature of 71°C.
8. Remove the cheese-crusted pork chops from the air fryer and let them rest for a few minutes before serving.
9. Serve the **cheese-crusted pork chops** with your choice of sides, such as roasted vegetables or a fresh salad.

Bacon Wrapped Pork with Apple Gravy

Serves: 4 | Prep & Cook time: 40 Min

- 4 pork tenderloin medallions (about 150g each)
- 8 slices of bacon
- 2 tablespoons olive oil
- 2 apples, peeled, cored, and diced
- 1 small onion, finely chopped
- 2 cloves of garlic, minced
- 250ml chicken or vegetable stock
- 2 tablespoons butter
- 2 tablespoons all-purpose flour
- Salt and pepper to taste

DIRECTIONS:

1. Wrap each pork tenderloin medallion with 2 slices of bacon, securing the bacon with toothpicks if needed.
2. Brush the bacon-wrapped pork with olive oil and season with salt and pepper.
3. Place the pork medallions in Zone 1 of the air fryer basket.
4. In Zone 2, add the diced apples, onion, and minced garlic. Toss to coat evenly.
5. Select Zone 1, choose the AIR FRY program, set the temperature to 200°C, and set the time to 25 minutes. Press the START/STOP button to begin cooking.
6. Select Zone 2, choose the ROAST program, set the temperature to 200°C, and set the time to 8-10 minutes. Press the START/STOP.
7. While the pork and apples are cooking, prepare the apple gravy. In a saucepan, melt the butter over medium heat. Add the flour and stir continuously for 1-2 minutes to make a roux.
8. Gradually whisk in the chicken or vegetable stock, cook for a few minutes until the mixture thickens.
9. Add the cooked apples, onion, and garlic from Zone 2 of the air fryer to the saucepan with the gravy. Stir well to combine. Season with salt and pepper to taste. Continue cooking the gravy over low heat for another 3-5 minutes, allowing the flavors to meld together.
10. Once the cooking time for the pork is complete, remove the **bacon-wrapped pork** medallions from Zone 1 of the air fryer and let them rest for a few minutes.
11. Drizzle the apple gravy over the pork chops and garnish with fresh chopped parsley. Enjoy!

Italian Sausage Links

Serves: 4 | Prep & Cook time: 25 Min

- 8 Italian sausage links
- 1 tablespoon olive oil
- 1 teaspoon dried oregano
- 1 teaspoon dried basil
- 1/2 teaspoon garlic powder
- 1/2 teaspoon onion powder
- Salt and pepper, to taste

DIRECTIONS:

1. In a small bowl, mix together the dried oregano, dried basil, garlic powder, onion powder, salt, and pepper.
2. Drizzle the olive oil over the Italian sausage links and rub them with the spice mixture to coat evenly.
3. Place the seasoned sausage links in Zone 1 of the air fryer. Select Zone 1, choose the AIR FRY program, set the temperature to 200°C, and set the time to 20 minutes. Press the START/STOP button to begin cooking.
4. After 10 minutes of cooking, carefully flip the sausage links using tongs to ensure even browning.
5. Once the cooking time is complete, remove the Italian sausage links from the air fryer.
6. Serve the **Italian sausage links** on a platter and enjoy them as they are, or use them in sandwiches, pasta dishes, or other recipes according to your preference.

These Italian Sausage Links prepared in the Ninja Dual Zone air fryer will be deliciously seasoned and have a crispy exterior. They can be enjoyed on their own or used in various dishes to add flavor and protein.

Meat & Rice Stuffed Peppers

Serves: 4 | Prep & Cook time: 40 Min

- 4 large bell peppers (any color)
- 250g ground beef
- 1 small onion, finely chopped
- 1 garlic clove, minced
- 200g cooked rice
- 200g tomato passata
- 1 teaspoon dried oregano
- 1 teaspoon dried basil
- Salt and pepper, to taste
- 50g grated cheddar cheese.

DIRECTIONS:

1. Cut the tops off the bell peppers and remove the seeds and membranes. Set aside.
2. In a pan, cook the ground beef over medium heat until browned. Add the chopped onion and minced garlic, and cook until the onion is softened.
3. Add the cooked rice, tomato passata, dried oregano, dried basil, salt, and pepper to the pan. Stir well to combine all the ingredients and let the mixture simmer for a few minutes.
4. Spoon the meat and rice mixture into each bell pepper, filling them to the top.
5. Sprinkle grated cheddar cheese on top of each stuffed pepper.
6. Place the stuffed peppers in Zone 1 of the air fryer. Select Zone 1, choose the AIR FRY program, set the temperature to 180°C, and set the time to 20-25 minutes. Press the START/STOP button to begin cooking. Cook until the peppers are tender and the cheese is melted and golden.
7. Once cooked, remove the stuffed peppers from the air fryer and let them cool slightly before serving.
8. Serve the **Meat and Rice Stuffed Peppers** as a delicious main course. They can be enjoyed on their own or accompanied by a side salad or crusty bread.

Spicy Rump Steak

Serves: 4 | Prep & Cook time: 25 Min

- 4 rump steaks (approximately 200g each)
- 2 tablespoons olive oil
- 2 teaspoons paprika
- 1 teaspoon garlic powder
- 1 teaspoon onion powder
- 1 teaspoon cayenne pepper (adjust to taste)
- 1 teaspoon dried oregano
- 1 teaspoon dried thyme
- Salt and pepper, to taste
- Fresh parsley, for garnish (optional)

DIRECTIONS:

1. In a small bowl, mix together the paprika, garlic powder, onion powder, cayenne pepper, dried oregano, dried thyme, salt, and pepper to create a spice rub.
2. Rub the spice mixture onto both sides of each rump steak, ensuring they are evenly coated.
3. Drizzle the olive oil over the steaks and gently massage it into the meat.
4. Place the seasoned rump steaks in Zone 1 of the air fryer. (If too crowded, place and cook in both zone)
5. Select Zone 1, choose the ROAST program, set the temperature to 200°C, and set time to 10-15 minutes, depending on your desired level of doneness. Press the START/STOP button to begin cooking.
6. After 5-7 minutes, flip the steaks over using tongs to ensure even cooking.
7. Continue cooking for the remaining time or until the steaks reach your desired level of doneness. For medium-rare, aim for an internal temperature of 55-60°C. Adjust the cooking time accordingly if you prefer your steaks more or less cooked.
8. Once cooked, remove the steaks from the air fryer and let them rest for a few minutes before slicing.
9. Garnish with fresh parsley, if desired, and serve the **Spicy Rump Steaks** hot. They can be enjoyed on their own or served with a side of roasted vegetables, mashed potatoes, or a crisp salad.

Sumptuous Pizza Tortilla Rolls

Serves: 4 | Prep & Cook time: 25 Min

- 4 large flour tortillas
- 125 ml tomato sauce
- 100 g shredded mozzarella cheese
- 30 g sliced pepperoni
- 30 g sliced black olives
- 30 g sliced red bell pepper
- 30 g sliced mushrooms
- 1/4 teaspoon dried oregano
- 1/4 teaspoon garlic powder
- Salt and pepper, to taste.

DIRECTIONS:

1. Lay out one tortilla on a clean surface. Spread a thin layer of tomato sauce evenly over the tortilla, leaving a small border around the edges.
2. Sprinkle 25 g of shredded mozzarella cheese over the tomato sauce.
3. Add 7.5 g of pepperoni slices, black olives, red bell pepper, and mushrooms on top of the cheese.
4. Sprinkle a pinch of dried oregano, garlic powder, salt, and pepper over the toppings.
5. Roll up the tortilla tightly, starting from one end. Repeat the process for the remaining tortillas and fillings.
6. Place the tortilla rolls in both zone. Select Zone 1, then select the AIR FRY function. Set the temperature to 180°C and the time to 10 minutes. Select MACTH. Press the START/STOP button to begin cooking.
7. Flip the tortilla rolls halfway through the cooking time to ensure even browning.
8. Once the tortilla rolls are golden brown and crispy, remove them from the air fryer and let them cool slightly.
9. Cut each tortilla roll into bite-sized pieces and serve as a delicious appetizer or snack.
10. Enjoy the **sumptuous pizza tortilla rolls** !

Note: Feel free to customize the toppings according to your preferences. Adjust the cooking time if needed to achieve your desired level of crispness.

Bacon-Wrapped Cheese Pork

Serves: 4 | Prep & Cook time: 35 Min

- 4 boneless pork chops (about 150g each)
- 8 slices of bacon
- 100g cheddar cheese, cut into thin strips
- 1 teaspoon dried thyme
- 1/2 teaspoon garlic powder
- Salt and pepper, to taste
- Cooking oil spray

DIRECTIONS:

1. Preheat Zone 1 of the Ninja Dual Zone air fryer to 200°C for 5 minutes.
2. Meanwhile, season the pork chops with dried thyme, garlic powder, salt, and pepper. Wrap each pork chop with 2 slices of bacon, securing them with toothpicks if needed.
3. Place the bacon-wrapped pork chops in Zone 1 of the air fryer. Select Zone 1, choose the AIR FRY program, set the temperature to 200°C, and set the time to 15 minutes. Press the START/STOP button to begin cooking.
4. In the meantime, prepare the cheese filling. Take each pork chop and make a small incision in the side. Insert the thin strips of cheddar cheese into the incision, distributing evenly among the pork chops.
5. After 15 minutes of cooking, open the air fryer and carefully flip the bacon-wrapped pork chops using tongs. Return them to Zone 1 and continue cooking for an additional 5 minutes.
6. Once the cooking time is complete, remove the bacon-wrapped cheese pork from the air fryer. Allow them to rest for a few minutes before serving.
7. Serve the **Bacon-Wrapped Cheese Pork** hot with your choice of sides, such as mashed potatoes or a green salad.

Southern Chili

Serves: 4 | Prep & Cook time: 45 Min

- 500g ground beef
- 1 onion, diced
- 2 cloves of garlic, minced
- 1 red bell pepper, diced
- 1 can (400g) diced tomatoes
- 1 can (400g) kidney beans, drained and rinsed
- 1 tablespoon tomato paste
- 1 tablespoon chili powder
- 1 teaspoon ground cumin
- 1 teaspoon paprika
- 1/2 teaspoon dried oregano
- 1/2 teaspoon sugar
- Salt and pepper, to taste
- Optional toppings: grated cheese, sour cream, chopped green onions

DIRECTIONS:

1. In Zone 1 of the air fryer, add the ground beef, onion, garlic, and red bell pepper. Select Zone 1, choose the AIR FRY program, set the temperature to 200°C, and set the time to 10 minutes. Press the START/STOP button to begin cooking. Cook until the ground beef is browned and the vegetables are softened.
2. Drain any excess fat from the ground beef mixture.
3. In Zone 1 of the air fryer, keep adding the diced tomatoes, kidney beans, tomato paste, chili powder, ground cumin, paprika, dried oregano, sugar, salt, and pepper. Mix well.
4. Select Zone 1, choose the BAKE program, set the temperature to 180°C, and set the time to 20 minutes. Press the START/STOP button to begin cooking. Stir the chili mixture occasionally during cooking.
5. After 20 minutes of cooking, check the seasoning and adjust if needed.
6. Serve the **Southern Chili** hot, garnished with grated cheese, sour cream, and chopped green onions, if desired.

Bacon & Cheese Stuffed Pork Chops

Serves: 4 | Prep & Cook time: 40 Min

- 4 boneless pork chops
- 4 slices of bacon
- 100g grated cheddar cheese
- 1 teaspoon dried thyme
- 1 teaspoon paprika
- Salt and pepper, to taste
- 1 tablespoon olive oil.

DIRECTIONS:

1. In a bowl, combine the grated cheddar cheese, dried thyme, paprika, salt, and pepper.
2. Using a sharp knife, make a deep pocket in each pork chop by cutting horizontally through the side.
3. Stuff each pork chop pocket with the cheese mixture.
4. Wrap each stuffed pork chop with a slice of bacon, securing it with toothpicks if necessary.
5. Brush the pork chops with olive oil on both sides.
6. Place the bacon-wrapped pork chops in Zone 1 of the air fryer. Select Zone 1, choose the AIR FRY program, set the temperature to 200°C, and set the time to 20-25 minutes. Press the START/STOP button to begin cooking. Cook until the pork chops are browned and cooked through, with an internal temperature of 70°C.
7. Once cooked, remove the pork chops from the air fryer and let them rest for a few minutes before serving.
8. Serve the **Bacon and Cheese Stuffed Pork Chops** hot, alongside your favorite side dishes like roasted vegetables, mashed potatoes, or a fresh salad.

Beef Mince Taco Rolls

Serves: 4 | Prep & Cook time: 30 Min

- 500g beef mince
- 1 small onion, finely diced
- 2 cloves garlic, minced
- 2 teaspoons chili powder
- 1 teaspoon ground cumin
- 1 teaspoon paprika
- 1/2 teaspoon dried oregano
- Salt and pepper, to taste
- 4 large tortilla wraps
- 100g grated cheddar cheese
- Salsa, sour cream, and guacamole, for serving
- Fresh coriander (cilantro), for garnish (optional)

DIRECTIONS:

1. In a large skillet or frying pan, heat a little oil over medium heat. Add the diced onion and minced garlic, and cook until softened and translucent.
2. Add the beef mince to the pan and cook until browned, breaking it up with a spatula or spoon as it cooks.
3. Stir in the chili powder, ground cumin, paprika, dried oregano, salt, and pepper. Cook for another 2-3 minutes to allow the flavors to meld.
4. Remove the beef mince mixture from the heat and set aside.
5. Place one tortilla wrap on a clean surface. Spoon a portion of the beef mince mixture onto the center of the tortilla, spreading it out evenly.
6. Sprinkle grated cheddar cheese over the beef mince mixture.
7. Roll up the tortilla tightly, folding in the sides as you go. Repeat this process for the remaining tortillas and filling.
8. Place the taco rolls in Zone 1 of the air fryer. Select Zone 1, choose the AIR FRY program, set temperature to 180°C, and set time to 15 minutes. Press the START/STOP button to begin cooking.
9. After 6-8 minutes, flip the taco rolls over. Continue cooking for the remaining time or until the taco rolls are crispy and golden.
10. Once cooked, remove the taco rolls from the air fryer and let them cool for a few minutes.
11. Serve the **Beef Mince Taco Rolls** with salsa, sour cream, guacamole, and fresh coriander for garnish.

Pork Kebab with Yogurt Sauce

Serves: 4 | Prep & Cook time: 35 Min

For the Pork Kebabs:
- 500g pork tenderloin, cut into cubes
- 1 red onion, cut into chunks
- 1 red bell pepper, cut into chunks
- 1 green bell pepper, cut into chunks
- 2 tablespoons olive oil
- 2 tablespoons lemon juice
- 2 cloves garlic, minced
- 1 teaspoon ground cumin
- 1 teaspoon paprika
- 1/2 teaspoon dried oregano
- Salt and pepper, to taste
- Skewers (if using wooden skewers, soak them in water for 30 minutes before use)

For the Yogurt Sauce:
- 200g Greek yogurt
- 1 tablespoon lemon juice
- 1 tablespoon chopped fresh mint
- Salt and pepper, to taste

DIRECTIONS:

1. In a bowl, combine the olive oil, lemon juice, minced garlic, ground cumin, paprika, dried oregano, salt, and pepper. Mix well to create a marinade.
2. Add the pork tenderloin cubes to the marinade and toss to coat them evenly. Let the pork marinate for at least 10 minutes to absorb the flavors.
3. Thread the marinated pork cubes onto skewers, alternating with chunks of red onion and bell peppers.
4. Place the pork kebabs in Zone 1 of the air fryer. Select Zone 1, choose the AIR FRY program, set the temperature to 200°C, and set time to 15 minutes. Press the START/STOP button to begin cooking. (If too crowded, place and cook in both zone). After 8 minutes, flip the kebabs rolls over.
5. While the kebabs are cooking, prepare the yogurt sauce. In a small bowl, combine the Greek yogurt, lemon juice, chopped fresh mint, salt, and pepper. Stir well to combine.
6. Once the kebabs are cooked and nicely browned, remove them from the air fryer.
7. Serve the **Pork Kebabs hot with the yogurt sauce** on the side.

Marinated Steak Tips with Mushrooms

Serves: 4 | Prep & Cook time: 80 Min

- 500g steak tips, cut into bite-sized pieces
- 200g mushrooms, sliced
- 3 tablespoons olive oil
- 2 tablespoons Worcestershire sauce
- 2 tablespoons soy sauce
- 2 tablespoons balsamic vinegar
- 2 cloves garlic, minced
- 1 teaspoon Dijon mustard
- 1 teaspoon dried thyme
- Salt and pepper, to taste
- Fresh parsley, chopped (for garnish)

DIRECTIONS:

1. In a bowl, combine the olive oil, Worcestershire sauce, soy sauce, balsamic vinegar, minced garlic, Dijon mustard, dried thyme, salt, and pepper. Mix well to make the marinade.
2. Place the steak tips in a shallow dish and pour the marinade over them. Make sure the steak tips are well coated. Cover the dish and marinate in the refrigerator for at least 1 hour, or overnight for best flavor.
3. In Zone 1, place the marinated steak tips along with the mushrooms. Reserve any remaining marinade for later use.
4. Select Zone 1, select the ROAST function, and at 200°C, set the cooking time to 12 minutes. Press the START/STOP button to begin cooking.
5. While the steak tips are cooking, you can heat the reserved marinade in a small saucepan over medium heat until it comes to a simmer. Let it simmer for a few minutes to thicken slightly.
6. Once the cooking time is complete, carefully remove the steak tips and mushrooms from the air fryer.
7. Serve the marinated steak tips and mushrooms on a plate, drizzle with the heated marinade, and garnish with freshly chopped parsley.
8. Enjoy the flavorful **Marinated Steak Tips with Mushrooms** with your favorite side dishes or a fresh salad.

Cheese Pork Chops

Serves: 4 | Prep & Cook time: 25 Min

- 4 pork chops
- 100g grated cheddar cheese
- 2 tablespoons breadcrumbs
- 1 tablespoon olive oil
- 1 teaspoon dried thyme
- 1/2 teaspoon garlic powder
- Salt and pepper, to taste

DIRECTIONS:

1. Preheat the Ninja Dual Zone Air Fryer by selecting Zone 1, then selecting the AIR FRY function. Set the temperature to 180°C and the time to 3 minutes. Press the START/STOP button to begin preheating.
2. In a shallow dish, combine the grated cheddar cheese, breadcrumbs, dried thyme, garlic powder, salt, and pepper.
3. Brush the pork chops with olive oil on both sides.
4. Dip each pork chop into the cheese and breadcrumb mixture, pressing firmly to coat both sides evenly.
5. Once the air fryer has preheated, place the pork chops in Zone 1. Select Zone 1, then select the AIR FRY function. Set the temperature to 180°C and the time to 12-15 minutes. Press the START/STOP button to begin cooking.
6. Flip the pork chops halfway through the cooking time to ensure even browning and cooking.
7. Cook the pork chops until they reach an internal temperature of 63°C and the cheese is melted and golden brown.
8. Once cooked, remove the pork chops from the air fryer and let them rest for a few minutes before serving.
9. Serve the **cheese pork chops** with your choice of sides, such as roasted vegetables, mashed potatoes, or a fresh salad.

Chicken Fried Steak with Cream Gravy

Serves: 4 | Prep & Cook time: 30 Min

For the Chicken Fried Steak:

- 4 beef cube steaks
- 100g all-purpose flour
- 1 teaspoon paprika
- 1/2 teaspoon garlic powder
- 1/2 teaspoon onion powder
- 1/2 teaspoon dried thyme
- Salt and pepper, to taste
- 2 eggs, beaten
- Vegetable oil, for frying

For the Cream Gravy:

- 2 tablespoons butter
- 2 tablespoons all-purpose flour
- 250ml whole milk
- Salt and pepper, to taste

DIRECTIONS

1. In a shallow dish, combine the all-purpose flour, paprika, garlic powder, onion powder, dried thyme, salt, and pepper.
2. Dip each beef cube steak into the beaten eggs, then coat it in the flour mixture, pressing firmly to adhere the coating to the steak. Repeat the process for all the steaks.
3. Once the air fryer has preheated, place the coated steaks in Zone 1. Select Zone 1, then select the AIR FRY function. Set the temperature to 200°C and the time to 15 minutes. Press the START/STOP button to begin cooking (if coated steaks don't fit in zone 1, use cook on both zones, don't forget to use the MATCH button).
4. While the steaks are cooking, prepare the cream gravy. In a saucepan, melt the butter over medium heat. Add the all-purpose flour and cook for 1-2 minutes, stirring constantly, until the mixture turns golden brown.
5. Gradually whisk in the whole milk, ensuring there are no lumps. Cook the mixture, stirring constantly, until the gravy thickens. Season with salt and pepper to taste. Remove from heat and set aside.
6. Flip the steaks halfway through the cooking time to ensure even browning and cooking.
7. Once the steaks are cooked and golden brown, remove them from the air fryer and let them rest for a few minutes.
8. Serve the chicken fried steaks with the cream gravy poured over the top. They are traditionally enjoyed with mashed potatoes and steamed vegetables.
9. Enjoy the comforting and delicious **chicken fried steak with creamy gravy**!

Bean & Beef Meatball Taco Pizza

Serves: 4 | Prep & Cook time: 35 Min

For the Meatballs:

- 300g lean ground beef
- 60g breadcrumbs
- 25g grated Parmesan cheese
- 25g finely chopped onion
- 1 clove garlic, minced
- 1 teaspoon dried oregano
- 1/2 teaspoon ground cumin
- Salt and pepper, to taste

For the Taco Pizza:

- 4 small tortillas
- 120g refried beans
- 60g grated cheddar cheese
- 60g diced tomatoes
- 30g sliced black olives
- 15g chopped fresh cilantro
- Sour cream and salsa, for serving

DIRECTIONS

1. In a mixing bowl, combine the ground beef, breadcrumbs, Parmesan cheese, onion, garlic, dried oregano, ground cumin, salt, and pepper. Mix well until all ingredients are evenly incorporated.
2. Shape the meat mixture into small meatballs, about 2.5cm in diameter. Place the meatballs in Zone 1 of the air fryer. Select Zone 1, choose the AIR FRY program, set the temperature to 200°C, and set the time to 10 minutes. Press the START/STOP.
3. While the meatballs are cooking, prepare the taco pizza. Take each tortilla and spread a layer of refried beans on one side.
4. Place the tortillas with the refried beans in Zone 2.
5. Select Zone 2, choose the AIR FRY program, set the temperature to 180°C, and time to 5 minutes. Press the START/STOP.
6. After 5 minutes, open the air fryer and remove the tortillas with the refried beans from Zone 2. Sprinkle grated cheddar cheese, diced tomatoes, sliced black olives, and chopped cilantro on top of the tortillas.
7. Return the tortillas with the toppings to Zone 2 and continue cooking for an additional 5 minutes or until the cheese has melted and the tortillas are crispy.
8. Once the cooking time is complete, remove the taco pizzas and meatballs from the air fryer.
9. Serve the **Bean and Beef Meatball Taco Pizza** hot, topped with the cooked meatballs. Garnish with sour cream and salsa, if desired.

Roast Beef with Horseradish Cream

Serves: 6 | Prep & Cook time: 55 Min

- 1.2 kg beef roast (such as topside, sirloin, or rib-eye)
- 2 tablespoons olive oil
- 1 tablespoon Dijon mustard
- 2 cloves garlic, minced
- 1 tablespoon fresh rosemary, chopped
- Salt and pepper, to taste

For the Horseradish Cream:

- 200g sour cream
- 2 tablespoons prepared horseradish
- 1 tablespoon fresh lemon juice
- Salt and pepper, to taste

For serving:

- Roasted vegetables (such as potatoes, carrots, and parsnips)
- Fresh parsley, for garnish

DIRECTIONS

1. In a small bowl, combine the olive oil, Dijon mustard, minced garlic, chopped rosemary, salt, and pepper.
2. Place the beef roast in both zone of the air fryer.
3. Spread the olive oil and mustard mixture evenly over the beef, coating it on all sides.
4. Select Zone 1, Select the ROAST, function, set the temperature to 200°C, and set the cooking time to 30-40 minutes, depending on your preferred level of doneness (30 minutes for medium-rare, 35 minutes for medium, or 40 minutes for medium-well). Select MATCH to duplicate settings across both zones. Press the START/STOP button to begin cooking.
5. While the beef is cooking, prepare the horseradish cream. In a bowl, combine the sour cream, horseradish, lemon juice, salt, and pepper. Mix well to combine.
6. Once the beef is cooked to your desired level, remove it from the air fryer and let it rest for a few minutes before slicing.
7. Slice the **roast beef** and serve it with roasted vegetables and a dollop of **horseradish cream**. Garnish with fresh parsley.

Note: Cooking times may vary depending on the size and thickness of your beef roast. It's recommended to use a meat thermometer to ensure the desired level of doneness.

Salmon on Bed of Fennel & Carrot

Serves: 2 | Prep & Cook time: 35 Min

- 2 salmon fillets (about 150g each)
- 1 fennel bulb, thinly sliced
- 2 carrots, julienned
- 2 tablespoons olive oil
- 2 cloves garlic, minced
- 1 lemon, zest and juice
- 1 teaspoon dried dill
- Salt and pepper, to taste
- Chopped fresh dill, for garnish.

DIRECTIONS:

1. In Zone 1, place the thinly sliced fennel and julienned carrots. Drizzle with olive oil and sprinkle with minced garlic, dried dill, salt, and pepper. Toss to coat the vegetables evenly.
2. Select Zone 1, select the ROAST function, setting the temperature to 200°C and set the cooking time to 15 minutes. Press the START/STOP button to begin roasting the vegetables.
3. While the vegetables are roasting, season the salmon fillets with salt, pepper, and lemon zest on both sides.
4. Place the seasoned salmon fillets in Zone 2 of the air fryer. Select Zone 2, select the ROAST function, setting the temperature to 200°C and set the cooking time to 10 minutes. Press the START/STOP button to begin roasting the salmon fillets.
5. Halfway through the cooking process, drizzle the salmon fillets with lemon juice for added flavor.
6. Once the vegetables are tender and the salmon fillets are cooked through and flaky, remove them from the air fryer.
7. Serve the roasted salmon fillets on a plate on top of the bed of roasted fennel and carrot. Garnish with chopped fresh dill.
8. Enjoy the delightful and healthy **Salmon on Bed of Fennel and Carrot.**

Garlic Lemon Scallops

Serves: 4 | Prep & Cook time: 20 Min

- 500g scallops
- 2 tablespoons butter, melted
- 2 cloves garlic, minced
- Zest of 1 lemon
- Juice of 1 lemon
- 2 tablespoons chopped fresh parsley
- Salt and pepper, to taste
- Lemon wedges, for serving.

DIRECTIONS:

1. In a bowl, combine the melted butter, minced garlic, lemon zest, lemon juice, chopped parsley, salt, and pepper.
2. Pat dry the scallops with a paper towel to remove excess moisture.
3. Place the scallops in Zone 1 of the air fryer.
4. Drizzle the butter mixture over the scallops, ensuring they are evenly coated.
5. Select Zone 1, select the AIR FRY function, setting the temperature to 200°C and set the cooking time to 10 minutes. Press the START/STOP button to begin cooking the scallops.
6. Halfway through the cooking process, gently flip the scallops to ensure even browning.
7. Once the scallops are golden brown and cooked through, remove them from the air fryer.
8. Serve the Garlic Lemon Scallops on a platter, garnished with fresh parsley and accompanied by lemon wedges.
9. Enjoy the delicious and flavorful **Garlic Lemon Scallops!**

Chapter 6: Fish & Seafood

Crispy Fish Sticks

Serves: 4 | Prep & Cook time: 27 Min

- 500g white fish fillets (such as cod or haddock), cut into finger-sized strips
- 100g all-purpose flour
- 2 eggs, beaten
- 150g breadcrumbs
- 1 teaspoon paprika
- 1/2 teaspoon garlic powder
- Salt and pepper to taste
- Lemon wedges, for serving
- Tartar sauce or ketchup, for dipping.

DIRECTIONS:

1. Place the flour, beaten eggs, and breadcrumbs in separate shallow bowls. Season the flour with salt, pepper, paprika, and garlic powder, and mix well.
2. Dip each fish strip into the seasoned flour, shaking off any excess.
3. Dip the floured fish strip into the beaten eggs, allowing any excess to drip off.
4. Coat the fish strip with breadcrumbs, pressing gently to adhere.
5. Repeat the coating process for the remaining fish strips.
6. Place the coated fish sticks in Zone 1 of the air fryer. Select Zone 1, select the AIR FRY function, set temperature to 200°C and cooking time 12 minutes. Press the START/STOP to begin cooking.
7. Halfway through the cooking process, carefully flip the fish sticks to ensure even browning.
8. Once the cooking time is complete, remove the fish sticks from the air fryer and let them cool slightly before serving.
9. Serve the crispy fish sticks with lemon wedges and your choice of tartar sauce or ketchup for dipping.
10. Enjoy the delicious and **crispy fish sticks** as a snack, appetizer, or main dish.

Sole & Cauliflower Fritters

Serves: 2 | Prep & Cook time: 30 Min

- 200g sole fillets, boneless and skinless
- 200g cauliflower florets
- 1 small onion, finely chopped
- 2 cloves garlic, minced
- 2 tablespoons fresh parsley, finely chopped
- 1 teaspoon lemon zest
- 2 eggs, beaten
- 50g breadcrumbs
- Salt and pepper to taste
- Vegetable oil spray.

DIRECTIONS:

1. Steam the cauliflower florets until tender. Drain and allow them to cool.
2. In a food processor, pulse the sole fillets, steamed cauliflower, chopped onion, minced garlic, fresh parsley, and lemon zest until well combined but still slightly chunky.
3. Transfer the mixture to a bowl and add the beaten eggs, breadcrumbs, salt, and pepper. Mix until everything is evenly incorporated.
4. Shape the mixture into small fritters, about the size of a golf ball.
5. Place the fritters in Zone 1 of the air fryer. Select Zone 1, select the AIR FRY function, set temperature to 200°C, set the cooking time to 10 minutes. Press the START/STOP.
6. Halfway through the cooking process, carefully flip the fritters to ensure even browning.
7. Once the cooking time is complete, remove the fritters from the air fryer and let them cool slightly before serving.
8. Lightly spray the fritters with vegetable oil spray to enhance their crispiness.
9. Serve the sole and cauliflower fritters as a delicious and nutritious appetizer or main dish.
10. You can accompany the fritters with a side of mixed greens or a dip of your choice, such as tartar sauce or lemon aioli.
11. This recipe for **sole and cauliflower fritters** is tailored to the taste preferences of the UK people, who enjoy flavorful and crispy fritters.

Prawn Dejonghe Skewers

Serves: 4 | Prep & Cook time: 30 Min

- 500g large prawns, peeled and deveined
- 4 cloves garlic, minced
- 2 tablespoons fresh parsley, finely chopped
- 2 tablespoons breadcrumbs
- 2 tablespoons grated Parmesan cheese
- 2 tablespoons melted butter
- 1 tablespoon lemon juice
- Salt and pepper to taste
- Vegetable oil spray
- Skewers (soaked in water if using wooden skewers)

DIRECTIONS:

1. In a bowl, combine the minced garlic, fresh parsley, breadcrumbs, grated Parmesan cheese, melted butter, lemon juice, salt, and pepper. Mix well to create a flavorful coating.
2. Thread the prawns onto the skewers, ensuring they are evenly spaced.
3. Brush the prawns generously with the garlic and parsley mixture, coating them on all sides.
4. Place the prawn skewers in Zone 1 of the air fryer. Select Zone 1, select the AIR FRY function, set temperature to 200°C and the cooking time to 10 minutes. Press the START/STOP button to begin cooking.
5. Halfway through the cooking process, carefully flip the skewers to ensure even cooking and browning.
6. Once the prawns are cooked through and the coating is crispy and golden, remove the skewers from the air fryer.
7. Lightly spray the prawns with vegetable oil spray for added crispiness, if desired.
8. Serve the **Prawn Dejonghe Skewers** as an appetizer or main dish, accompanied by a side of lemon wedges and your favorite dipping sauce.
9. Enjoy the succulent prawns with the flavorful garlic and parsley coating!

Butter-Wine Baked Salmon

Serves: 4 | Prep & Cook time: 35 Min

- 4 salmon fillets (about 150g each)
- 4 tablespoons unsalted butter, melted
- 3 tablespoons white wine
- 2 cloves garlic, minced
- 2 tablespoons fresh lemon juice
- 1 tablespoon chopped fresh dill
- Salt and pepper to taste
- Lemon slices and fresh dill sprigs for garnish.

DIRECTIONS:

1. In a small bowl, mix together the melted butter, white wine, minced garlic, fresh lemon juice, chopped dill, salt, and pepper.
2. Place the salmon fillets in a shallow baking dish or foil-lined tray.
3. Pour the butter-wine mixture over the salmon fillets, ensuring they are evenly coated.
4. Place the baking dish or tray with the salmon fillets in Zone 1 of the air fryer. Select Zone 1, select the AIR FRY function, set temperature to 180°C and set the cooking time to 15 minutes. Press the START/STOP button to begin cooking.
5. Halfway through the cooking process, baste the salmon fillets with the butter-wine mixture to keep them moist and flavorful.
6. Continue cooking until the salmon is cooked through and flakes easily with a fork.
7. Once done, carefully remove the salmon fillets from the air fryer and transfer them to a serving platter.
8. Garnish with fresh dill sprigs and lemon slices.
9. Serve the **Butter-Wine Baked Salmon** with your choice of sides, such as roasted vegetables or a fresh salad.
10. Enjoy the succulent and flavorful salmon!

Foil-Packet Lobster Tail

Serves: 2 | Prep & Cook time: 20 Min

- 2 lobster tails
- 2 tablespoons unsalted butter, melted
- 2 cloves garlic, minced
- 1 tablespoon fresh lemon juice
- Salt and pepper, to taste
- Fresh parsley, chopped (for garnish)
- Lemon wedges (for serving)

DIRECTIONS:

1. Using kitchen shears, carefully cut through the top shell of each lobster tail lengthwise, stopping before the tail fins.
2. Gently lift the lobster meat from the shell, keeping it attached at the base, and place it on top of the shell.
3. In a small bowl, combine the melted butter, minced garlic, and lemon juice. Season with salt and pepper to taste.
4. Brush the garlic butter mixture generously over each lobster tail, making sure to coat all exposed meat.
5. Place each lobster tail on a separate piece of foil. Fold up the edges of the foil to create a packet, leaving a small vent on top to allow steam to escape.
6. Place the foil packets with the lobster tails in Zone 1 of the Ninja Dual Zone air fryer.
7. Select Zone 1, select the AIR FRY function, set temperature to 200°C and set the cooking time to 12 minutes . Press the START/STOP button to begin cooking.
8. While the lobster tails are cooking, you can prepare any side dishes or sauces to accompany the meal.
9. Once the cooking time is complete, carefully open the foil packets (watch out for steam) and transfer the lobster tails to serving plates.
10. Garnish with freshly chopped parsley and serve with lemon wedges on the side.
11. Enjoy the **Foil-Packet Lobster Tails** while they're hot and tender!

Scallops with Asparagus & Peas

Serves: 4 | Prep & Cook time: 20 Min

- 16 large scallops
- 200g asparagus spears, trimmed
- 200g fresh or frozen peas
- 2 tablespoons olive oil
- 2 cloves garlic, minced
- 1 lemon, zest and juice
- Salt and pepper, to taste
- Fresh parsley, for garnish

DIRECTIONS:

1. In a mixing bowl, combine the asparagus spears, peas, olive oil, minced garlic, lemon zest, salt, and pepper. Toss to coat the vegetables evenly.
2. Once the air fryer is preheated, place the seasoned vegetables in Zone 1 and arrange the scallops in Zone 2 of the air fryer.
3. Select zone 1, select AIR FRY and set temperature to 200°C and set time to 10 minutes. Select MATCH to duplicate settings across both zones. Press the START/STOP button to begin cooking.
4. Cook for 5 minutes, then carefully flip the scallops and stir the vegetables.
5. Continue cooking for another 5 minutes or until the scallops are opaque and cooked through, and the vegetables are tender-crisp.
6. Once cooked, remove the scallops and vegetables from the air fryer. Squeeze fresh lemon juice over the scallops and vegetables.
7. Serve the **scallops on a plate with the asparagus and pea** mixture. Garnish with fresh parsley.

Paprika Prawns

Serves: 2 | Prep & Cook time: 20 Min

- 300g large prawns, peeled and deveined.
- 2 tablespoons olive oil
- 1 teaspoon smoked paprika
- 1/2 teaspoon garlic powder
- 1/4 teaspoon cayenne pepper (optional, for added heat)
- 1/2 teaspoon salt
- 1/4 teaspoon black pepper
- Fresh lemon wedges, for serving
- Chopped parsley, for garnish.

DIRECTIONS:

1. In a bowl, combine the olive oil, smoked paprika, garlic powder, cayenne pepper (if using), salt, and black pepper. Mix well.
2. Add the prawns to the bowl and toss until they are coated evenly with the spice mixture.
3. Place the prawns in Zone 1 of the air fryer. Select Zone 1, select the AIR FRY function, setting the temperature to 200°C and set the cooking time to 10 minutes. Press the START/STOP button to begin cooking.
4. Halfway through the cooking process, shake the air fryer basket to ensure even cooking.
5. Once the prawns are cooked and turn pink, remove them from the air fryer and transfer to a serving dish.
6. Squeeze fresh lemon juice over the prawns and garnish with chopped parsley.
7. Serve the Paprika Prawns as an appetizer or main dish with your favorite dipping sauce or alongside a fresh salad or rice.
8. Enjoy the delicious and flavorful **Paprika Prawns!**

Roasted Cod with Lemon-Garlic Potatoes

Serves: 2 | Prep & Cook time: 35 Min

- 2 cod fillets (about 150g each)
- 300g baby potatoes, halved
- 2 tablespoons olive oil
- 2 cloves garlic, minced
- 1 lemon, zest and juice
- 1 teaspoon dried thyme
- Salt and pepper, to taste
- Chopped fresh parsley, for garnish.

DIRECTIONS:

1. In a bowl, combine the olive oil, minced garlic, lemon zest, lemon juice, dried thyme, salt, and pepper. Mix well.
2. Add the halved baby potatoes to the bowl and toss until they are coated evenly with the marinade.
3. Place the marinated potatoes in Zone 1 of the air fryer. Select Zone 1, select the ROAST function, set temperature to 200°C and the cooking time to 15 minutes. Press the START/STOP button to begin roasting the potatoes.
4. While the potatoes are roasting, season the cod fillets with salt and pepper on both sides.
5. Place the seasoned cod fillets to Zone 2 of the air fryer. Select Zone 2, select the ROAST function, set temperature to 200°C and set the cooking time to 10 minutes. Press the START/STOP button to begin roasting the cod fillets.
6. Halfway through the cooking process, flip the cod fillets to ensure even cooking.
7. Once the potatoes are golden and crispy, and the cod fillets are cooked through and flaky, remove them from the air fryer.
8. Serve the roasted cod fillets on a plate alongside the lemon-garlic potatoes. Garnish with chopped fresh parsley.
9. Enjoy the delicious and satisfying **Roasted Cod with Lemon-Garlic Potatoes!**

Browned Prawns Patties

Serves: 4 | Prep & Cook time: 30 Min

- 500g (1.1 lbs) prawns, peeled and deveined
- 1 small onion, finely chopped
- 2 cloves garlic, minced
- 25g breadcrumbs
- 2 tablespoons mayonnaise
- 1 tablespoon Worcestershire sauce
- 1 tablespoon Dijon mustard
- 1 tablespoon chopped fresh parsley
- 1/2 teaspoon salt
- 1/4 teaspoon black pepper
- 2 tablespoons vegetable oil.

DIRECTIONS:

1. In a food processor, add the prawns and pulse until coarsely chopped. Transfer the chopped prawns to a mixing bowl.
2. To the bowl with the prawns, add the chopped onion, minced garlic, breadcrumbs, mayonnaise, Worcestershire sauce, Dijon mustard, chopped fresh parsley, salt, and black pepper. Mix well to combine all the ingredients.
3. Form the mixture into patties, approximately 8 patties of equal size.
4. Once Zone 1 is preheated, lightly brush the air fryer basket in Zone 1 with vegetable oil. Place the prawn patties in Zone 1's cooking basket in a single layer.
5. Select Zone 1, choosing AIR FRY, set the temperature to 200°C, and set the cooking time to 10-12 minutes. Press the START/STOP button to begin cooking.
6. While the patties are cooking, you can prepare a sauce or a side salad to accompany the prawn patties.
7. After the cooking time is complete, carefully remove the browned prawn patties from the air fryer.
8. Serve the **Browned Prawn Patties** hot, either on their own or in burger buns with your preferred condiments.

Lemon Pepper Prawns

Serves: 2 | Prep & Cook time: 25 Min

- 300g (10.5oz) large prawns, peeled and deveined
- 2 tablespoons olive oil
- 1 lemon (zest and juice)
- 1 teaspoon ground black pepper
- 1/2 teaspoon salt
- 1 teaspoon dried parsley
- 1/2 teaspoon garlic powder
- Optional: Fresh parsley, chopped (for garnish)

DIRECTIONS:

1. In a bowl, combine the olive oil, lemon zest, lemon juice, black pepper, salt, dried parsley, and garlic powder. Mix well to create a marinade.
2. Add the prawns to the marinade and toss them to coat evenly. Allow the prawns to marinate for 10 minutes.
3. Once Zone 1 is preheated, place the marinated prawns in Zone 1's cooking basket in a single layer.
4. Select Zone 1, choosing AIR FRY, set the temperature to 200°C and set the cooking time to 10 minutes. Press the START/STOP button to begin cooking.
5. While the prawns are cooking, you can prepare a side salad or your preferred accompaniment.
6. After the cooking time is complete, carefully remove the cooked prawns from the air fryer.
7. Serve the Lemon Pepper Prawns immediately. You can garnish them with fresh chopped parsley, if desired.
8. Enjoy the flavorful and succulent **Lemon Pepper Prawns**!

Nutty Prawns with Amaretto Glaze

Serves: 10 | Prep & Cook time: 25 Min

- 1 kg prawns, peeled and deveined
- 100 g breadcrumbs
- 50 g finely chopped mixed nuts (such as almonds, walnuts, and cashews)
- 25 g grated Parmesan cheese
- 2 tablespoons fresh parsley, chopped
- 2 tablespoons olive oil
- 2 tablespoons Amaretto liqueur
- 1 tablespoon lemon juice
- 2 cloves garlic, minced
- Salt and pepper, to taste
- Lemon wedges, for serving.

DIRECTIONS:

1. In a shallow bowl, combine the breadcrumbs, mixed nuts, Parmesan cheese, and chopped parsley.
2. In another bowl, whisk together the olive oil, Amaretto liqueur, lemon juice, minced garlic, salt, and pepper.
3. Dip each prawn into the olive oil mixture, allowing any excess to drip off.
4. Coat the prawns in the breadcrumb and nut mixture, pressing gently to adhere.
5. Place the coated prawns in both zone of the air fryer.
6. Select zone 1, select AIR FRY and set temperature to 200°C and set time to 10 minutes. Select MATCH to duplicate settings across both zones. Press the START/STOP button to begin cooking.
7. Halfway through the cooking process, gently shake the basket to ensure even cooking of the prawns.
8. Once the prawns are golden brown and cooked through, remove them from the air fryer.
9. Serve the **Nutty Prawns with Amaretto Glaze** on a platter, accompanied by lemon wedges for squeezing over the prawns.
10. Enjoy the delightful combination of crunchy nutty coating and the sweet Amaretto glaze on the succulent prawns!

Crab-Stuffed Avocado Boats

Serves: 4 | Prep & Cook time: 20 Min

- 2 ripe avocados
- 200g crabmeat
- 2 tablespoons mayonnaise
- 1 tablespoon lemon juice
- 2 tablespoons chopped fresh parsley
- 2 tablespoons chopped fresh chives
- 1/4 teaspoon garlic powder
- Salt and pepper, to taste
- Lemon wedges, for serving.

DIRECTIONS:

1. Cut the avocados in half lengthwise and remove the pits. Scoop out a little bit of flesh from each half to create a cavity for the stuffing. Chop the scooped-out avocado and set aside.
2. In a bowl, combine the crabmeat, mayonnaise, lemon juice, chopped parsley, chopped chives, garlic powder, salt, and pepper. Mix well.
3. Gently fold in the chopped avocado into the crab mixture.
4. Spoon the crab mixture into the hollowed-out avocado halves, mounding it up.
5. Place the stuffed avocado halves in Zone 1 of the air fryer.
6. Select Zone 1, select the AIR FRY function, set temperature to 180°C and set the cooking time to 8 minutes. Press the START/STOP button to begin cooking.
7. Once the cooking is complete, remove the Crab-Stuffed Avocado Boats from the air fryer.
8. Serve the avocado boats on a platter, garnished with additional chopped parsley and lemon wedges on the side.
9. Enjoy the creamy and flavorful **Crab-Stuffed Avocado Boats**!
10. Please note that the cooking times may vary depending on the size and ripeness of the avocados. Adjust the cooking time accordingly to achieve the desired level of doneness.

Garlic Butter Prawns Scampi

Serves: 4 | Prep & Cook time: 20 Min

- 500g large prawns, peeled and deveined
- 4 tablespoons unsalted butter, melted
- 4 cloves garlic, minced
- 2 tablespoons chopped fresh parsley
- 1 tablespoon lemon juice
- Salt and pepper, to taste
- Lemon wedges, for serving.

DIRECTIONS:

1. In a bowl, combine the melted butter, minced garlic, chopped parsley, lemon juice, salt, and pepper. Mix well.
2. Add the peeled and deveined prawns to the bowl and toss to coat them evenly with the garlic butter mixture.
3. Place the prawns in Zone 1 of the air fryer in a single layer.
4. Select Zone 1, select the AIR FRY function, setting the temperature to 200°C and set the cooking time to 10 minutes. Press the START/STOP button to begin cooking.
5. Halfway through the cooking time, gently shake or flip the prawns to ensure even cooking.
6. Once the cooking is complete, remove the Garlic Butter Prawns Scampi from the air fryer.
7. Serve the prawns on a platter, garnished with additional chopped parsley and lemon wedges on the side.
8. Enjoy the succulent and flavorful **Garlic Butter Prawns Scampi**.
9. Note: Cooking times may vary depending on the size and thickness of the prawns. Adjust the cooking time accordingly to ensure they are cooked through and opaque.

Moroccan Spiced Halibut with Chickpea Salad

Serves: 2 | Prep & Cook time: 30 Min

- 2 halibut fillets (about 150g each)
- 1 teaspoon ground cumin
- 1 teaspoon ground coriander
- 1/2 teaspoon ground paprika
- 1/2 teaspoon ground cinnamon
- 1/4 teaspoon cayenne pepper (adjust to taste)
- Salt and pepper, to taste
- 2 tablespoons olive oil

For the Chickpea Salad:
- 200g canned chickpeas, drained and rinsed
- 1/2 red onion, finely chopped
- 1/2 cucumber, diced
- 1 large tomato, diced
- 4 tablespoons chopped fresh parsley
- 1 tablespoon lemon juice
- 1 tablespoon extra-virgin olive oil
- Salt and pepper, to taste.

DIRECTIONS:

1. In a small bowl, mix together the ground cumin, ground coriander, ground paprika, ground cinnamon, cayenne pepper, salt, and pepper.
2. Rub the spice mixture all over the halibut fillets.
3. Place the seasoned halibut fillets in Zone 1 of the air fryer.
4. Select Zone 1, select the AIR FRY function, temperature to 200°C and set the cooking time to 15 minutes. Press the START/STOP button to begin cooking.
5. In the meantime, prepare the chickpea salad. In a mixing bowl, combine the drained and rinsed chickpeas, chopped red onion, diced cucumber, diced tomato, chopped parsley, lemon juice, extra-virgin olive oil, salt, and pepper. Mix well.
6. Once the cooking is complete, remove the halibut fillets from the air fryer. They should be flaky and cooked through.
7. Serve the Moroccan Spiced Halibut on a plate, accompanied by a generous serving of the chickpea salad.
8. Enjoy the delightful flavors of the **Moroccan Spiced Halibut with Chickpea Salad!**

Fish Cakes

Serves: 4 | Prep & Cook time: 35 Min

- 400g white fish fillets (such as cod or haddock)
- 500g potatoes, peeled and diced
- 1 small onion, finely chopped
- 2 tablespoons chopped fresh parsley
- 1 tablespoon lemon juice
- 1 teaspoon Dijon mustard
- Salt and pepper to taste
- 2 eggs, beaten
- 100g breadcrumbs
- Vegetable oil, for brushing.

DIRECTIONS:

1. Place the fish fillets in Zone 1 of the air fryer. Select Zone 1, select the AIR FRY function, set the temperature to 200°C and set the time to 10 minutes. Press the START/STOP. Once cooked, remove the fish fillets from the air fryer and let them cool slightly.
2. Meanwhile, boil the diced potatoes in a pot of salted water until tender. Drain and mash the potatoes.
3. In a bowl, flake the cooked fish fillets into small pieces. Add the mashed potatoes, chopped onion, parsley, lemon juice, Dijon mustard, salt, and pepper. Mix well to combine.
4. Shape the mixture into fish cakes of your desired size.
5. Dip each fish cake into the beaten eggs, then coat with breadcrumbs.
6. Place the fish cakes in Zone 1 of the air fryer. Select Zone 1, select the AIR FRY function, set the temperature to 200°C and set the time to 12-15 minutes. Press the START/STOP.
7. While the fish cakes are cooking, lightly brush them with vegetable oil halfway through the cooking process to promote browning and crispiness.
8. Once the cooking time is complete, remove the fish cakes from the air fryer and let them cool slightly before serving.
9. Serve the **fish cakes** hot with tartar sauce or a squeeze of lemon juice. They can be enjoyed with a side of salad or steamed vegetables.

Thai Fishcakes

Serves: 2 | Prep & Cook time: 25 Min

- 300g skinless white fish fillets (such as cod or pollock)
- 1 egg
- 1 heaped tablespoon Thai red curry paste
- 4 fresh lime leaves, finely shredded, lightly beaten
- 1 teaspoon light brown soft sugar
- 2 teaspoons fish sauce
- 50g green beans, finely sliced
- 1 tablespoon finely chopped coriander
- 1 tablespoon sunflower oil
- 100g cucumber, sliced
- 1 little gem lettuce, roughly chopped
- 3 tablespoons sweet chilli sauce.

DIRECTIONS:

1. Roughly chop the fish and place in a food processor. Pulse briefly until roughly chopped. Add the red curry paste, lime leaves, egg, sugar and fish sauce and whizz until just combined. Tip into a bowl and stir through the beans and coriander.
2. Shape the mixture into 6 fishcakes. Brush all over with the oil and place in zone 1 drawer (with crisper plate inserted), then insert drawer in unit. Select zone 1, select AIR FRY and set temperature to 200°C and set time to 10 minutes. Press the START/STOP button to begin cooking.
3. When zone 1 time reaches 5 minutes, remove drawer from unit and turn the fishcakes using silicone-tipped tongs. Reinsert drawer to continue cooking.
4. When cooking is complete serve 3 **fishcakes** per person, with the cucumber and lettuce and the sweet chilli sauce alongside.

Cooked Tuna with Lemongrass

Serves: 4 | Prep & Cook time: 27 Min

- 4 tuna steaks
- 2 stalks lemongrass, white part only, finely chopped
- 2 cloves garlic, minced
- 2 tablespoons soy sauce
- 1 tablespoon fish sauce
- 1 tablespoon lime juice
- 1 tablespoon vegetable oil
- Salt and pepper to taste
- Fresh cilantro for garnish (optional)

DIRECTIONS:

1. In a bowl, combine the chopped lemongrass, minced garlic, soy sauce, fish sauce, lime juice, vegetable oil, salt, and pepper. Mix well to create the marinade.
2. Place the tuna steaks in a shallow dish and0 pour the marinade over them. Make sure the tuna steaks are coated evenly. Allow them to marinate for at least 10 minutes.
3. Then place marinated tuna steaks in zone 1.
4. Select Zone 1, select the AIR FRY function, temperature to 200°C and set the cooking time to 12 minutes. Press the START/STOP button to begin cooking
5. Cook the tuna steaks for about 5-6 minutes per side, or until desired doneness. The internal temperature should reach 54-57°C for medium-rare.
6. Once cooked, remove the tuna steaks from the heat and let them rest for a few minutes.
7. Serve the **Cooked Tuna with Lemongrass** hot, garnished with fresh cilantro if desired. They pair well with steamed rice or a fresh salad.

Miso Salmon

Serves: 2 | Prep & Cook time: 25 Min

- 2 salmon fillets
- 2 tablespoons white miso paste
- 1 tablespoon honey
- 1 tablespoon soy sauce
- 1 tablespoon rice vinegar
- 1 teaspoon grated fresh ginger
- 1 clove garlic, minced
- 1 tablespoon vegetable oil
- Sesame seeds, for garnish
- Sliced spring onions, for garnish.

DIRECTIONS:

1. In a small bowl, whisk together the miso paste, honey, soy sauce, rice vinegar, grated ginger, minced garlic, and vegetable oil to make the marinade.
2. Place the salmon fillets in a shallow dish or a resealable plastic bag. Pour the marinade over the salmon, ensuring it is well-coated. Let it marinate for about 10 minutes.
3. Remove the salmon fillets from the marinade, reserving the marinade for later use.
4. Place the salmon fillets on the grill grate or in the cooking basket of Zone 1.
5. Select Zone 1, select the AIR FRY function, temperature to 200°C and set the cooking time to 10 minutes. Press the START/STOP button to begin cooking.
6. While the salmon is cooking, transfer the reserved marinade to a small saucepan. Bring it to a boil over medium heat, then reduce the heat and simmer for a few minutes until it thickens slightly.
7. Once the salmon is cooked and flakes easily with a fork, remove it from the air fryer.
8. Drizzle the cooked salmon with the thickened marinade.
9. Garnish with sesame seeds and sliced spring onions.
10. Serve the **Miso Salmon** hot with steamed rice or a side of vegetables.

Note: Adjust the cooking time based on the thickness of the salmon fillets.

Breaded Prawns Tacos

Serves: 8 tacos | Prep & Cook time: 25 Min

- 300g prawns, peeled and deveined
- 100g all-purpose flour
- 2 eggs, beaten
- 100g breadcrumbs
- 1 teaspoon paprika
- 1/2 teaspoon garlic powder
- 1/2 teaspoon salt
- 1/4 teaspoon black pepper
- 8 small flour tortillas.
- 50 grams shredded lettuce
- 75 grams diced tomatoes
- 30 grams diced red onion
- Fresh cilantro leaves (for garnish)
- Lime wedges (for serving)
- Your choice of sauce (such as tartar sauce or chili sauce)

DIRECTIONS

1. In three separate shallow bowls or plates, set up your breading station. In the first bowl, place the all-purpose flour. In the second bowl, beat the eggs. In the third bowl, combine the breadcrumbs, paprika, garlic powder, salt, and black pepper.
2. Take a prawn and dip it into the flour, coating it lightly. Shake off any excess flour.
3. Dip the floured prawn into the beaten eggs, ensuring it is coated evenly.
4. Transfer the prawn to the breadcrumb mixture and coat it well, pressing gently to adhere the breadcrumbs to the prawn. Repeat this process with the remaining prawns.
5. Lightly grease the cooking basket in Zone 1 of the Ninja Dual Zone Air Fryer with cooking spray or brush it with a small amount of oil.
6. Arrange the breaded prawns in a single layer in Zone 1's cooking basket. (If there are still breaded prawns, place them to zone 2)
7. Select Zone 1, choose the AIR FRY function, and set the temperature to 200°C. Set the cooking time to 10 minutes. (if place breaded prawns in both zone , Select MATCH). Press the START/STOP button to begin cooking.
8. While the prawns are cooking, warm the flour tortillas according to package instructions.
9. Once the prawns are cooked and golden brown, carefully remove them from the air fryer.
10. To assemble the tacos, place a tortilla on a flat surface. Add a layer of shredded lettuce, followed by a few breaded prawns. Top with diced tomatoes, diced red onion, and fresh cilantro leaves.
11. Serve the Breaded Prawns Tacos with lime wedges and your choice of sauce on the side.
12. Enjoy the delicious **Breaded Prawns Tacos** while they're still warm and crispy!

Thai Prawn Skewers with Peanut Dipping Sauce

Serves: 2 | Prep & Cook time: 30 Min

For the Prawn Skewers:
- 12 large prawns, peeled and deveined
- 2 tablespoons soy sauce
- 2 tablespoons fish sauce
- 2 tablespoons lime juice
- 1 tablespoon honey
- 1 tablespoon vegetable oil
- 2 cloves garlic, minced
- 1 tablespoon fresh coriander, chopped
- 1 red chili, seeded and finely chopped (optional)
- Bamboo skewers, soaked in water for 30 minutes.

For the Peanut Dipping Sauce:
- 3 tablespoons peanut butter
- 2 tablespoons soy sauce
- 1 tablespoon lime juice
- 1 tablespoon honey
- 1 teaspoon sesame oil
- Water (as needed to adjust consistency)
- Crushed peanuts, for garnish (optional)
- Fresh coriander, for garnish (optional)

DIRECTIONS

1. In a bowl, combine the soy sauce, fish sauce, lime juice, honey, vegetable oil, minced garlic, chopped coriander, and chopped red chili (if using). Mix well to make the marinade.
2. Add the prawns to the marinade and toss to coat them evenly. Allow the prawns to marinate for at least 15 minutes.
3. Thread the marinated prawns onto the soaked bamboo skewers.
4. Place the prawn skewers on the grill grate or in the cooking basket of Zone 1.
5. Select Zone 1, select the AIR FRY function, set the temperature to 180°C and set the cooking time to 10 minutes . Press the START/STOP button to begin cooking.
6. While the prawns are cooking, prepare the peanut dipping sauce. In a separate bowl, whisk together the peanut butter, soy sauce, lime juice, honey, and sesame oil. Add water gradually to achieve the desired consistency for dipping.
7. Once the prawns are cooked and have turned pink, remove them from the air fryer.
8. Serve the **Thai prawn skewers with the peanut dipping sauce** on the side.
9. Garnish with crushed peanuts and fresh coriander, if desired.
10. Note: Adjust the cooking time based on the size and thickness of the prawns. Ensure that the prawns are cooked through and opaque.

Spring Rolls

Serves: 6 rolls | Prep & Cook time: 35 Min

- 6 spring roll wrappers
- 150g bean sprouts
- 100g shredded cabbage
- 100g shredded carrots
- 50g sliced mushrooms
- 50g sliced bell peppers
- 2 cloves garlic, minced
- 1 tablespoon soy sauce
- 1 tablespoon oyster sauce
- 1 teaspoon sesame oil
- 1 teaspoon cornstarch
- Vegetable oil, for brushing.

DIRECTIONS:

1. In a large bowl, combine the bean sprouts, cabbage, carrots, mushrooms, bell peppers, garlic, soy sauce, oyster sauce, sesame oil, and cornstarch. Mix well to coat the vegetables evenly.
2. Take one spring roll wrapper and place it on a clean surface. Spoon about 2-3 tablespoons of the vegetable filling onto the lower third of the wrapper.
3. Fold the sides of the wrapper over the filling, then roll tightly from the bottom, sealing the edges with a bit of water to secure the roll. Repeat this process with the remaining wrappers and filling.
4. Evenly dividing them between the two zone. Brush the spring rolls with a little vegetable oil on all sides.
5. Select zone 1, select AIR FRY and set temperature to 180°C and set time to 14 minutes (or until they are crispy and golden brown). Select MATCH to duplicate settings across both zones. Press the START/STOP button to begin cooking.
6. Once cooked, remove the **spring rolls** from the air fryer and let them cool for a few minutes. Serve the spring rolls with a dipping sauce of your choice, such as sweet chili sauce or soy sauce.

Prawn Toast

Serves: 2 | Prep & Cook time: 25 Min

- 200g raw prawns, peeled and deveined
- 2 slices white bread, crusts removed
- 1 spring onion, finely chopped
- 1 garlic clove, minced
- 1 teaspoon grated fresh ginger
- 1 tablespoon cornflour
- 1 tablespoon light soy sauce
- 1/2 teaspoon sesame oil
- Vegetable oil, for brushing
- Sesame seeds, for garnish
- Sweet chili sauce, for dipping.

DIRECTIONS:

1. In a food processor, blend the prawns, spring onion, garlic, ginger, cornflour, soy sauce, and sesame oil until you have a smooth paste.
2. Spread the prawn mixture evenly on the bread slices, pressing it down gently.
3. Cut each bread slice into 4 triangles.
4. Lightly brush the tops of the prawn toasts with vegetable oil and sprinkle sesame seeds on top.
5. Place the prawn toasts in Zone 1 of the Ninja Dual Zone Air Fryer.
6. Select zone 1, select AIR FRY and set temperature to 180°C and set time to 8-10 minutes (until golden and crispy). Press the START/STOP button to begin cooking.
7. Remove the prawn toasts from the air fryer and allow them to cool slightly.
8. Serve the **prawn toasts** with sweet chili sauce for dipping.

Chapter 7: Appetizers & Snacks

Baked Spanakopita Dip

Serves: 2 | Prep & Cook time: 35 Min

- 200g frozen spinach, thawed and drained
- 100g feta cheese, crumbled
- 50g cream cheese
- 25g grated Parmesan cheese
- 2 cloves garlic, minced
- 1/2 teaspoon dried dill
- 1/4 teaspoon salt
- 1/4 teaspoon black pepper
- 2 tablespoons olive oil

DIRECTIONS:

1. In a mixing bowl, combine the thawed and drained spinach, crumbled feta cheese, cream cheese, grated Parmesan cheese, minced garlic, dried dill, salt, black pepper, and olive oil. Mix well to combine all the ingredients.
2. Transfer the mixture to an oven-safe baking dish that fits inside the air fryer basket.
3. Place the baking dish in the air fryer basket in the Zone 1 cooking area.
4. Select zone 1, select BAKE and set temperature to 180°C and set time to 16-20 minutes. Press the START/STOP button to begin cooking.
5. Once the cooking time is complete, carefully remove the baking dish from the air fryer using oven mitts or heat-resistant gloves.
6. Serve the **Baked Spanakopita Dip** hot, alongside pita bread, tortilla chips, or your preferred dipping accompaniment.

Parmesan French Fries

Serves: 2 | Prep & Cook time: 30 Min

- 4 medium-sized potatoes
- 2 tablespoons olive oil
- 25g grated Parmesan cheese
- 1 teaspoon garlic powder
- 1/2 teaspoon paprika
- 1/2 teaspoon dried thyme
- 1/2 teaspoon salt
- 1/4 teaspoon black pepper
- Fresh parsley, chopped (for garnish)

DIRECTIONS:

1. Wash and peel the potatoes. Cut them into thin, evenly-sized French fry shapes.
2. In a large bowl, toss the potato fries with olive oil until they are evenly coated.
3. In a separate bowl, combine the grated Parmesan cheese, garlic powder, paprika, dried thyme, salt, and black pepper.
4. Sprinkle the Parmesan cheese mixture over the oiled potato fries and toss until the fries are well-coated with the seasoning.
5. Lightly grease the cooking basket in two zone of the Ninja Dual Zone Air Fryer with cooking spray or brush it with a small amount of oil.
6. Arrange the seasoned potato fries in a single layer in both zone cooking basket.
7. Select Zone 1, choose the AIR FRY function, and set the temperature to 200°C. Set the cooking time to 18-22 minutes. Select MATCH. Press the START/STOP button to begin cooking.
8. Halfway through the cooking time, pause the air fryer and shake the baskets to ensure even cooking. Then, continue cooking until the fries are crispy and golden brown.
9. Once the cooking time is complete, carefully remove the basket from the air fryer.
10. Sprinkle the **Parmesan French Fries** with fresh chopped parsley for added freshness and flavor. Serve immediately as a delicious side dish or snack.

Mexican Jalapeno Poppers

Serves: 4 | Prep & Cook time: 25 Min

- 8 jalapeno peppers
- 100g cream cheese, softened
- 50g cheddar cheese, grated
- 1/2 teaspoon ground cumin
- 1/2 teaspoon paprika
- 1/4 teaspoon garlic powder
- Salt and pepper, to taste
- 50g breadcrumbs
- Cooking spray or a small amount of oil, for greasing.

DIRECTIONS:

1. Cut each jalapeno pepper in half lengthwise and remove the seeds and membranes.
2. In a mixing bowl, combine the softened cream cheese, grated cheddar cheese, ground cumin, paprika, garlic powder, salt, and pepper. Mix well until all ingredients are incorporated.
3. Fill each jalapeno half with the cheese mixture, dividing it equally among them.
4. Lightly grease Zone 1 of the air fryer with cooking spray or a small amount of oil.
5. Place the stuffed jalapeno poppers in Zone 1 of the Ninja Dual Zone Air Fryer, ensuring they are in a single layer and not touching each other.
6. Select Zone 1, choose the AIR FRY program, and set the temperature to 180°C. Set the time to 10-12 minutes.
7. Press the START/STOP button to begin cooking in Zone 1.
8. After 5-6 minutes of cooking, pause the air fryer, open it, and carefully flip the jalapeno poppers in Zone 1.
9. Close the air fryer and resume cooking until the poppers are golden brown and the cheese is melted and bubbly.
10. Once cooked, remove the **jalapeno poppers** from Zone 1 and transfer them to a serving dish.

Crab Cake Poppers

Serves: 6 | Prep & Cook time: 25 Min

- 200g crab meat (fresh or canned)
- 1 small red bell pepper, finely chopped
- 1 small onion, finely chopped
- 1 celery stalk, finely chopped
- 2 tablespoons mayonnaise
- 1 tablespoon Dijon mustard
- 1 tablespoon Worcestershire sauce
- 1 teaspoon Old Bay seasoning (or a seafood seasoning blend)
- 1/2 teaspoon paprika
- 1/2 teaspoon garlic powder
- 50g breadcrumbs
- 1 egg, beaten
- Salt and pepper, to taste
- Cooking spray or a small amount of oil, for greasing.

DIRECTIONS:

1. In a mixing bowl, combine the crab meat, red bell pepper, onion, celery, mayonnaise, Dijon mustard, Worcestershire sauce, Old Bay seasoning, paprika, garlic powder, breadcrumbs, beaten egg, salt, and pepper. Mix well until all ingredients are evenly incorporated.
2. Shape the mixture into small bite-sized balls or patties.
3. Lightly grease Zone 1 of the air fryer with cooking spray or a small amount of oil.
4. Place the crab cake poppers in Zone 1 of the Ninja Dual Zone Air Fryer, making sure they are in a single layer and not touching each other. (If they are too crowded, divide them and place them in 2 cooking zones)
5. Select Zone 1, choose the AIR FRY program, and set the temperature to 200°C. Set the time to 10-12 minutes.
6. Press the START/STOP button to begin cooking.
7. After 5 minutes of cooking, pause the air fryer, open it, and carefully flip the crab cake poppers for even browning.
8. Close the air fryer and resume cooking until the crab cake poppers are golden brown and cooked through.
9. Once cooked, remove the **crab cake poppers** from air fryer and transfer them to a serving dish.

Fried Halloumi Cheese

Serves: 4 | Prep & Cook time: 15 Min

- 200g halloumi cheese, cut into slices or sticks
- 2 tablespoons plain flour
- 1 teaspoon paprika
- 1/2 teaspoon garlic powder
- Pinch of black pepper
- Cooking spray or a small amount of oil, for greasing.

DIRECTIONS:

1. In a shallow bowl, combine the plain flour, paprika, garlic powder, and black pepper.
2. Lightly grease Zone 1 of the air fryer with cooking spray or a small amount of oil.
3. Dip each halloumi slice or stick into the flour mixture, making sure it's coated on all sides.
4. Place the coated halloumi cheese in Zone 1 of the Ninja Dual Zone Air Fryer, ensuring they are in a single layer and not touching each other.
5. Select Zone 1, choose the AIR FRY program, and set the temperature to 200°C. Set the time to 8-10 minutes.
6. Press the START/STOP button to begin cooking in Zone 1.
7. After 4-5 minutes of cooking, pause the air fryer, open it, and carefully flip the halloumi cheese in Zone 1.
8. Close the air fryer and resume cooking until the halloumi cheese is golden brown and crispy.
9. Once cooked, remove the **fried halloumi cheese** from Zone 1 and transfer it to a serving plate.

Cauliflower Gnocchi

Serves: 4 | Prep & Cook time: 35 Min

- 500g cauliflower florets
- 150g plain flour
- 1 egg
- 1/2 teaspoon salt
- 1/4 teaspoon garlic powder
- Cooking spray or a small amount of oil, for greasing.

DIRECTIONS:

1. Steam the cauliflower florets until they are tender. Allow them to cool slightly.
2. Transfer the steamed cauliflower florets to a clean kitchen towel and squeeze out any excess moisture.
3. In a large mixing bowl, mash the cauliflower using a fork or potato masher until it resembles a rice-like texture.
4. Add the plain flour, egg, salt, and garlic powder to the mashed cauliflower. Mix well until a dough forms.
5. Divide the dough into small portions and roll each portion into a sausage-like shape.
6. Cut the rolled dough into bite-sized pieces to form the gnocchi.
7. Lightly grease Zone 1 of the air fryer with cooking spray or a small amount of oil.
8. Place the cauliflower gnocchi in Zone 1 of the Ninja Dual Zone Air Fryer, ensuring they are in a single layer and not touching each other.
9. Select Zone 1, choose the AIR FRY program, and set the temperature to 200°C. Set the time to 12-15 minutes.
10. Press the START/STOP button to begin cooking.
11. After 6-8 minutes of cooking, pause the air fryer, open it, and carefully shake or flip the cauliflower gnocchi in Zone 1.
12. Close the air fryer and resume cooking until the cauliflower gnocchi is golden brown and crispy.
13. Once cooked, remove the **cauliflower gnocchi** from Zone 1 and transfer them to a serving dish.

Pickle Chips

Serves: 4 | Prep & Cook time: 25 Min

- 400g dill pickle chips (sliced pickles)
- 100g all-purpose flour
- 2 large eggs, beaten
- 100g breadcrumbs
- 1 teaspoon paprika
- 1/2 teaspoon garlic powder
- 1/2 teaspoon dried dill
- 1/2 teaspoon salt
- 1/4 teaspoon black pepper
- Cooking spray or oil for greasing.

DIRECTIONS:

1. Pat dry the pickle chips using a paper towel to remove excess moisture.
2. Set up a breading station: In one bowl, place the all-purpose flour. In another bowl, beat the eggs. In a third bowl, combine the breadcrumbs, paprika, garlic powder, dried dill, salt, and black pepper.
3. Take a pickle chip and dip it into the flour, coating it lightly. Shake off any excess flour.
4. Dip the floured pickle chip into the beaten eggs, ensuring it is coated evenly.
5. Transfer the pickle chip to the breadcrumb mixture and coat it well, pressing gently to adhere the breadcrumbs to the pickle chip. Repeat this process with the remaining pickle chips.
6. Lightly grease the cooking basket in both zone of the Ninja Dual Zone Air Fryer with cooking spray or brush it with a small amount of oil.
7. Arrange the breaded pickle chips in a single layer in two zone s cooking basket.
8. Select Zone 1, choose the AIR FRY function, and set the temperature to 200°C. Set the cooking time to 8-10 minutes. Select MATCH. Press the START/STOP button to begin cooking.
9. Halfway through the cooking time, pause the air fryer and shake the baskets to ensure even cooking. Then, continue cooking until the pickle chips are golden brown and crispy.
10. Once the cooking time is complete, carefully remove the basket from the air fryer.
11. Serve the **Pickle Chips** immediately as a delicious appetizer or snack

Sweet Potato Fries with Mayonnaise

Serves: 2 | Prep & Cook time: 30 Min

- 2 medium-sized sweet potatoes
- 2 tablespoons cornstarch
- 1 tablespoon olive oil
- 1/2 teaspoon paprika
- 1/2 teaspoon garlic powder
- 1/2 teaspoon salt
- 1/4 teaspoon black pepper
- Cooking spray or oil for greasing
- Mayonnaise, for serving.

DIRECTIONS:

1. Wash and peel the sweet potatoes. Cut them into thin, even-sized strips to resemble fries.
2. In a large bowl, combine the cornstarch, paprika, garlic powder, salt, and black pepper. Toss the sweet potato fries in the cornstarch mixture until they are evenly coated.
3. Drizzle the olive oil over the coated sweet potato fries and toss to ensure the fries are well-coated.
4. Lightly grease the cooking basket in Zone 1 of the Ninja Dual Zone Air Fryer with cooking spray or brush it with a small amount of oil.
5. Arrange the sweet potato fries in a single layer in Zone 1 cooking basket.
6. Select Zone 1, choose the AIR FRY function, and set the temperature to 200°C. Set the cooking time to 20 minutes. Press the START/STOP button to begin cooking.
7. Halfway through the cooking time, pause the air fryer and shake the basket to ensure even cooking. Then, continue cooking until the sweet potato fries are crispy and golden brown.
8. Once the cooking time is complete, carefully remove the basket from the air fryer.
9. Serve the **Sweet Potato Fries** immediately with a side of mayonnaise for dipping.

Crispy Chilli Chickpeas

Serves: 4 | Prep & Cook time: 20 Min

- 2 cans (400g each) chickpeas, drained and rinsed
- 2 tablespoons olive oil
- 1 teaspoon smoked paprika
- 1/2 teaspoon ground cumin
- 1/2 teaspoon garlic powder
- 1/4 teaspoon cayenne pepper (adjust according to spice preference)
- 1/2 teaspoon salt
- 1/4 teaspoon black pepper
- Freshly squeezed lemon juice, for serving
- Chopped fresh cilantro, for garnish (optional)

DIRECTIONS:

1. In a bowl, combine the chickpeas, olive oil, smoked paprika, ground cumin, garlic powder, cayenne pepper, salt, and black pepper. Toss well to coat the chickpeas evenly with the spices.
2. Lightly grease the cooking basket in Zone 1 of the Ninja Dual Zone Air Fryer with cooking spray or brush it with a small amount of oil.
3. Place the seasoned chickpeas in Zone 1's cooking basket in a single layer.
4. Select Zone 1, choose the AIR FRY function, and set the temperature to 200°C. Set the cooking time to 15 minutes. Press the START/STOP button to begin cooking.
5. Halfway through the cooking time, pause the air fryer and shake the basket to ensure even cooking. Then, continue cooking until the chickpeas are crispy and golden brown.
6. Once the cooking time is complete, carefully remove the basket from the air fryer.
7. Squeeze some fresh lemon juice over the crispy chickpeas for added tanginess.
8. Sprinkle with chopped fresh cilantro if desired. Serve the **Crispy Chilli Chickpeas** as a delicious and healthy snack.

Tangy Fried Pickle Spears

Serves: 6 | Prep & Cook time: 25 Min

- 400g dill pickle spears
- 65g all-purpose flour
- 80g cornmeal
- 1 teaspoon paprika
- 1/2 teaspoon garlic powder
- 1/4 teaspoon cayenne pepper (adjust according to spice preference)
- 1/2 teaspoon salt
- 1/4 teaspoon black pepper
- 2 large eggs
- 2 tablespoons milk
- Cooking spray or oil for greasing
- Ranch dressing or dipping sauce of your choice, for serving.

DIRECTIONS:

1. In a shallow dish, combine the all-purpose flour, cornmeal, paprika, garlic powder, cayenne pepper, salt, and black pepper. Mix well.
2. In a separate bowl, whisk together the eggs and milk.
3. Lightly grease the cooking basket in Zone 1 of the Ninja Dual Zone Air Fryer with cooking spray or brush it with a small amount of oil.
4. Dip each pickle spear into the egg mixture, allowing any excess to drip off, then coat it with the flour mixture. Repeat for all pickle spears.
5. Place the breaded pickle spears in Zone 1's cooking basket in a single layer.
6. Select Zone 1, choose the AIR FRY function, and set the temperature to 200°C. Set the cooking time to 10 minutes. Press the START/STOP button to begin cooking.
7. Halfway through the cooking time, pause the air fryer and shake the basket to ensure even cooking. Then, continue cooking until the pickle spears are golden brown and crispy.
8. Once the cooking time is complete, carefully remove the basket from the air fryer.
9. Serve the **Tangy Fried Pickle Spears** hot with ranch dressing or your preferred dipping sauce.

Chilli-Brined Fried Calamari

Serves: 2 | Prep & Cook time: 80 Min

- 250g calamari rings
- 480g buttermilk
- 1 tablespoon hot sauce
- 1 teaspoon paprika
- 1/2 teaspoon garlic powder
- 1/2 teaspoon salt
- 1/4 teaspoon black pepper
- 100g all-purpose flour
- Cooking spray or oil for greasing
- Lemon wedges, for serving.

DIRECTIONS:

1. In a bowl, combine the buttermilk, hot sauce, paprika, garlic powder, salt, and black pepper. Stir well to mix the ingredients.
2. Add the calamari rings to the buttermilk mixture, ensuring they are fully submerged. Cover the bowl and refrigerate for at least 1 hour to allow the calamari to marinate.
3. In a shallow dish, place the all-purpose flour.
4. Remove the marinated calamari rings from the buttermilk mixture, allowing any excess liquid to drip off.
5. Dredge the calamari rings in the flour, coating them evenly. Shake off any excess flour.
6. Lightly grease the cooking basket in Zone 1 of the Ninja Dual Zone Air Fryer with cooking spray or brush it with a small amount of oil.
7. Arrange the breaded calamari rings in a single layer in Zone 1's cooking basket. (if leftovers, put them in zone 2 and cook on both zones)
8. Select Zone 1, choose the AIR FRY function, and set the temperature to 200°C. Set the cooking time to 8-10 minutes. Press the START/STOP button to begin cooking.
9. Halfway through the cooking time, pause the air fryer and shake the basket to ensure even cooking. Then, continue cooking until the calamari rings are golden brown and crispy.
10. Once the cooking time is complete, carefully remove the basket from the air fryer.
11. Serve the **Chilli-Brined Fried Calamari** immediately with lemon wedges for squeezing over the calamari.

Roasted Grape Dip

Serves: 6 | Prep & Cook time: 25 Min

- 500g seedless grapes
- 2 tablespoons olive oil
- 1 tablespoon honey
- 200g cream cheese, softened
- 200g Greek yogurt
- 1 teaspoon lemon juice
- 1/2 teaspoon dried thyme
- 1/4 teaspoon salt
- 1/4 teaspoon black pepper
- Crackers or bread, for serving.

DIRECTIONS:

1. In a bowl, toss the grapes with olive oil and honey until they are well coated.
2. Lightly grease the cooking basket in Zone 1 of the Ninja Dual Zone Air Fryer with cooking spray or brush it with a small amount of oil.
3. Place the grape mixture in Zone 1's cooking basket in a single layer.
4. Select Zone 1, choose the ROAST function, and set the temperature to 200°C. Set the cooking time to 15 minutes. Press the START/STOP button to begin cooking.
5. While the grapes are roasting, in a separate bowl, combine the softened cream cheese, Greek yogurt, lemon juice, dried thyme, salt, and black pepper. Mix well until smooth and creamy.
6. Once the cooking time is complete, carefully remove the basket from the air fryer.
7. Allow the roasted grapes to cool slightly, then chop them into smaller pieces.
8. Add the chopped roasted grapes to the cream cheese mixture and stir until well combined.
9. Transfer the Roasted Grape Dip to a serving bowl. Serve the **Roasted Grape Dip** with crackers or bread.

Air Fried Pot Stickers | Makes 30 pot stickers

Serves: 4 | Prep & Cook time: 40 Min

- 30 round dumpling wrappers
- 300g ground pork
- 100g cabbage, finely chopped
- 50g spring onions, finely chopped
- 1 tablespoon soy sauce
- 1 tablespoon sesame oil
- 1/2 teaspoon grated ginger
- 1/2 teaspoon garlic powder
- 1/4 teaspoon black pepper
- Water, for sealing the pot stickers
- Soy sauce and vinegar, for dipping

DIRECTIONS:

1. In a large bowl, combine the ground pork, chopped cabbage, chopped spring onions, soy sauce, sesame oil, grated ginger, garlic powder, and black pepper. Mix well until all the ingredients are evenly incorporated.
2. Place a dumpling wrapper on a clean surface. Spoon about 1 tablespoon of the pork mixture onto the center of the wrapper.
3. Dip your finger into water and run it along the edge of the dumpling wrapper. Fold the wrapper in half, creating a half-moon shape, and press the edges firmly to seal the pot sticker. Repeat this process with the remaining wrappers and filling.
4. Lightly grease the cooking basket in Zone 1 with cooking spray or brush it with a small amount of oil.
5. Arrange the pot stickers in a single layer in Zone 1's cooking basket, ensuring they are not touching each other. (if there are leftovers, put them in zone 2 and cook on both zones)
6. Select Zone 1, choose the AIR FRY function, and set the temperature to 190°C. Set the cooking time to 10 minutes. Press the START/STOP.
7. Once the cooking time is complete, carefully remove the basket from the air fryer.
8. Serve the **Air Fried Pot Stickers** immediately with a dipping sauce made from soy sauce and vinegar.

Crispy Mozzarella Sticks

Serves: 4 | Prep & Cook time: 25 Min

- 200g mozzarella cheese, cut into sticks
- 100g all-purpose flour
- 2 large eggs, beaten
- 100g breadcrumbs
- 1 teaspoon dried oregano
- 1/2 teaspoon garlic powder
- 1/2 teaspoon paprika
- 1/4 teaspoon salt
- 1/4 teaspoon black pepper
- Cooking spray or oil for greasing
- Marinara sauce or any dipping sauce of your choice.

DIRECTIONS:

1. Set up a breading station: In one bowl, place the all-purpose flour. In another bowl, beat the eggs. In a third bowl, combine the breadcrumbs, dried oregano, garlic powder, paprika, salt, and black pepper.
2. Take a mozzarella stick and coat it in the flour, shaking off any excess.
3. Dip the floured mozzarella stick into the beaten eggs, ensuring it is coated evenly.
4. Transfer the mozzarella stick to the breadcrumb mixture and coat it well, pressing gently to adhere the breadcrumbs to the cheese. Repeat this process with the remaining mozzarella sticks.
5. Lightly grease the cooking basket in Zone 1 of the Ninja Dual Zone Air Fryer with cooking spray or brush it with a small amount of oil.
6. Arrange the breaded mozzarella sticks in a single layer in Zone 1's cooking basket.
7. Select Zone 1, choose the AIR FRY, set the temperature to 200°C. Set the cooking time to 8-10 minutes. Press the START/STOP.
8. Halfway through the cooking time, pause the air fryer and shake the basket to ensure even cooking. Then, continue cooking until the mozzarella sticks are golden brown and crispy.
9. Once the cooking time is complete, carefully remove the basket from the air fryer.
10. Serve **Crispy Mozzarella Sticks** immediately with marinara sauce or any dipping sauce of your choice.

Veggie Shrimp Toast

Serves: 4 | Prep & Cook time: 30 Min

- 200g cooked shrimp, peeled and chopped
- 1 small carrot, grated
- 1/2 small zucchini, grated
- 2 spring onions, finely chopped
- 2 tablespoons fresh cilantro, chopped
- 1 clove garlic, minced
- 1 teaspoon grated ginger
- 1 tablespoon soy sauce
- 1 teaspoon sesame oil
- 1/2 teaspoon salt
- 1/4 teaspoon black pepper
- 8 slices of bread
- Sesame seeds for garnish.

DIRECTIONS:

1. In a mixing bowl, combine the cooked shrimp, grated carrot, grated zucchini, chopped spring onions, fresh cilantro, minced garlic, grated ginger, soy sauce, sesame oil, salt, and black pepper. Mix well to combine all the ingredients.
2. Cut the slices of bread into quarters to form smaller triangles.
3. Spoon a generous amount of the shrimp and vegetable mixture onto each bread triangle, spreading it evenly.
4. Lightly grease the cooking basket in Zone 1 of the Ninja Dual Zone Air Fryer with cooking spray or a small amount of oil.
5. Place the shrimp toast triangles in Zone 1's cooking basket in a single layer.
6. Select Zone 1, choose the AIR FRY function, and set the temperature to 200°C. Set the cooking time to 10 minutes. Press the START/STOP.
7. Halfway through the cooking time, pause the air fryer and flip the shrimp toast triangles to ensure even browning. Then, continue cooking until they are crispy and golden brown.
8. Once the cooking time is complete, carefully remove the basket from the air fryer.
9. Garnish the Veggie Shrimp Toast with sesame seeds. Serve the **Veggie Shrimp Toast** as an appetizer or snack.

Garlic-Parmesan Croutons

Serves: 4 | Prep & Cook time: 20 Min

- 4 slices of bread, preferably a crusty variety like baguette or ciabatta
- 2 tablespoons olive oil
- 2 cloves garlic, minced
- 2 tablespoons grated Parmesan cheese
- 1/2 teaspoon dried Italian herbs
- Salt and pepper to taste.

DIRECTIONS:

1. Cut the bread slices into bite-sized cubes or desired crouton shapes.
2. In a mixing bowl, combine the olive oil, minced garlic, grated Parmesan cheese, dried Italian herbs, salt, and pepper. Mix well to create a flavorful seasoning mixture.
3. Add the bread cubes to the seasoning mixture and toss until they are well coated.
4. Lightly grease the cooking basket in Zone 1 of the Ninja Dual Zone Air Fryer with cooking spray or a small amount of oil.
5. Place the seasoned bread cubes in Zone 1's cooking basket in a single layer.
6. Select Zone 1, choose the AIR FRY function, and set the temperature to 180°C. Set the cooking time to 10 minutes. Press the START/STOP button to begin cooking.
7. Halfway through the cooking time, pause the air fryer and shake the basket to ensure even cooking. Then, continue cooking until the croutons are crispy and golden brown.
8. Once the cooking time is complete, carefully remove the basket from the air fryer.
9. Allow the croutons to cool slightly before serving. They will continue to crisp up as they cool.
10. Serve the **Garlic-Parmesan Croutons** on salads, soups, or enjoy them as a crunchy snack.

Easy Spiced Nuts

Serves: 4 | Prep & Cook time: 15 Min

- 200g mixed nuts (such as almonds, cashews, and walnuts)
- 1 tablespoon olive oil
- 1 tablespoon honey
- 1 teaspoon ground cinnamon
- 1/2 teaspoon ground cumin
- 1/4 teaspoon cayenne pepper (adjust according to spice preference)
- 1/2 teaspoon salt.

DIRECTIONS:

1. In a bowl, combine the mixed nuts, olive oil, honey, ground cinnamon, ground cumin, cayenne pepper, and salt. Toss well to coat the nuts evenly with the spice mixture.
2. Lightly grease the cooking basket in Zone 1 of the Ninja Dual Zone Air Fryer with cooking spray or a small amount of oil.
3. Place the spiced nuts in Zone 1's cooking basket in a single layer.
4. Select Zone 1, choose the AIR FRY function, and set the temperature to 180°C. Set the cooking time to 10 minutes. Press the START/STOP button to begin cooking.
5. Halfway through the cooking time, pause the air fryer and shake the basket to ensure even cooking. Then, continue cooking until the nuts are toasted and fragrant.
6. Once the cooking time is complete, carefully remove the basket from the air fryer.
7. Allow the spiced nuts to cool slightly before serving.
8. Serve the **Easy Spiced Nuts** as a tasty snack or appetizer.

Crispy Green Tomatoes with Horseradish

Serves: 4 | Prep & Cook time: 25 Min

- 4 green tomatoes
- 70g all-purpose flour
- 2 large eggs
- 100g breadcrumbs
- 25g grated Parmesan cheese
- 1/2 teaspoon paprika
- 1/2 teaspoon garlic powder
- Salt and pepper to taste
- 4 tablespoons horseradish sauce

DIRECTIONS:

1. Slice the green tomatoes into 1/4-inch thick rounds.
2. Place the flour in a shallow dish. In another shallow dish, whisk the eggs until well beaten. In a third shallow dish, combine the breadcrumbs, grated Parmesan cheese, paprika, garlic powder, salt, and pepper.
3. Dip each tomato slice into the flour, shaking off any excess. Then dip it into the beaten eggs, allowing any excess to drip off. Finally, coat the tomato slice in the breadcrumb mixture, pressing gently to adhere the coating.
4. Lightly grease the cooking basket in Zone 1 of the Ninja Dual Zone Air Fryer with cooking spray or a small amount of oil.
5. Place the coated tomato slices in Zone 1's cooking basket in a single layer.
6. Select Zone 1, choose the AIR FRY function, and set the temperature to 200°C. Set the cooking time to 10 minutes. Press the START/STOP button to begin cooking.
7. Halfway through the cooking time, pause the air fryer and flip the tomato slices to ensure even browning. Then, continue cooking until the tomatoes are crispy and golden brown.
8. Once the cooking time is complete, carefully remove the basket from the air fryer.
9. Serve the **Crispy Green Tomatoes** with a side of horseradish sauce for dipping.

Lemony Pear Chips

Serves: 4 | Prep & Cook time: 130 Min

- 2 large pears
- Juice of 1 lemon
- Zest of 1 lemon
- 2 tablespoons honey
- 1/2 teaspoon ground cinnamon.

DIRECTIONS:

1. Cut the pears into thin slices, about 1/8 inch thick. Remove any seeds or stems.
2. In a bowl, combine the lemon juice, lemon zest, honey, and ground cinnamon. Stir well to make a lemony marinade.
3. Place the pear slices in the marinade and gently toss them until they are evenly coated. Let them marinate for about 5 minutes.
4. Lightly grease the cooking basket in two zone of the Ninja Dual Zone Air Fryer with cooking spray or a small amount of oil.
5. Arrange the marinated pear slices in two zone cooking basket in a single layer, ensuring they do not overlap.
6. Select Zone 1, choose the DEHYDRATE function, and set the temperature to 80°C. Set the cooking time to 2 hours. Select MATCH. Press the START/STOP button to begin dehydrating.
7. After the first hour of cooking, pause the air fryer and flip the pear slices to ensure even dehydration. Then, continue dehydrating for the remaining hour.
8. Once the cooking time is complete, carefully remove the basket from the air fryer and let the pear chips cool completely. They will continue to crisp up as they cool.
9. Serve the **Lemony Pear Chips** as a healthy and flavorful snack.

Sea Salt Potato Crisps

Serves: 4 | Prep & Cook time: 30 Min

- 4 large potatoes (about 800g), preferably Maris Piper or King Edward
- 2 tablespoons olive oil
- Sea salt, to taste.

DIRECTIONS:

1. Wash and peel the potatoes. Slice them thinly, about 1/8 inch thick, using a sharp knife or a mandoline slicer.
2. Place the sliced potatoes in a large bowl of cold water and let them soak for 10 minutes. This helps remove excess starch and ensures crispy chips.
3. Drain the potatoes and pat them dry with a clean kitchen towel or paper towels.
4. In a separate bowl, toss the dried potato slices with olive oil until they are well coated.
5. Lightly grease the cooking basket in two zone of the Ninja Dual Zone Air Fryer with cooking spray or a small amount of oil.
6. Place the potato slices in both zone cooking basket in a single layer, ensuring they do not overlap.
7. Select Zone 1, choose the AIR FRY function, and set the temperature to 200°C. Set the cooking time to 15-20 minutes, depending on the desired level of crispiness. Select MATCH. Check the chips periodically and adjust the cooking time if needed.
8. Halfway through the cooking time, pause the air fryer and shake the basket to ensure even cooking. Then, continue cooking until the potato crisps are golden brown and crispy.
9. Once the cooking time is complete, carefully remove the basket from the air fryer. Sprinkle the hot potato crisps with sea salt, to taste.
10. Allow the potato crisps to cool slightly before serving. They will continue to crisp up as they cool.
11. Serve the **Sea Salt Potato Crisps** as a delicious snack or as a side dish to your favorite main course.

Crispy Filo Artichoke Triangles | Makes 18 Triangles

Serves: 4 | Prep & Cook time: 35 Min

- 200g canned artichoke hearts, drained and chopped
- 100g feta cheese, crumbled
- 50g grated Parmesan cheese
- 2 tablespoons chopped fresh dill
- 2 tablespoons chopped fresh parsley
- 1 teaspoon lemon zest
- Salt and pepper to taste
- 9 sheets of filo pastry
- Butter or cooking spray for greasing.

DIRECTIONS

1. In a bowl, combine the chopped artichoke hearts, crumbled feta cheese, grated Parmesan cheese, chopped fresh dill, chopped fresh parsley, lemon zest, salt, and pepper. Mix well to combine the filling ingredients.
2. Lay one sheet of filo pastry on a clean work surface and brush it lightly with melted butter or spray it with cooking spray. Place another sheet of filo pastry on top and repeat the process until you have a stack of three filo sheets.
3. Cut the filo stack into six equal squares.
4. Place a spoonful of the artichoke filling onto each filo square. Fold the filo square diagonal to form a triangle, enclosing the filling. Press the edges firmly to seal.
5. Repeat the process with the remaining filo sheets and filling until you have 18 filled triangles.
6. Lightly grease the cooking basket in two zone of the Ninja Dual Zone Air Fryer with cooking spray or brush it with a small amount of melted butter.
7. Place the filo triangles in both zone cooking basket in a single layer.
8. Select Zone 1, choose the AIR FRY function, and set the temperature to 200°C. Set the cooking time to 15 minutes. Select MATCH. Press the START/STOP.
9. Halfway through the cooking time, pause the air fryer and flip the filo triangles to ensure even browning. Then, continue cooking until the triangles are golden brown and crispy.
10. Once the cooking time is complete, carefully remove the basket from the air fryer.
11. Serve the **Crispy Filo Artichoke Triangles** as a delicious appetizer or snack.

Stuffed Bell Peppers

Serves: 4 | Prep & Cook time: 45 Min

- 4 bell peppers (any color)
- 200g lean ground beef
- 1 small onion, finely chopped
- 1 garlic clove, minced
- 200g cooked rice
- 200g canned diced tomatoes
- 50g grated cheddar cheese
- 1 teaspoon dried oregano
- 1/2 teaspoon paprika
- Salt and pepper, to taste
- Cooking spray or a small amount of oil, for greasing.

DIRECTIONS

1. Cut the tops off the bell peppers and remove the seeds and membranes. Trim the bottoms slightly, if needed, to help them stand upright in the air fryer.
2. In a skillet, cook the ground beef, onion, and garlic over medium heat until the beef is browned and the onion is softened. Drain any excess fat.
3. In a mixing bowl, combine the cooked ground beef mixture, cooked rice, diced tomatoes, grated cheddar cheese, dried oregano, paprika, salt, and pepper. Mix well.
4. Stuff each bell pepper with the mixture, dividing it equally among them.
5. Lightly grease both Zone of the air fryer with cooking spray or a small amount of oil.
6. Place the stuffed bell peppers in two zone (2 stuffed bell peppers in each zone) of the Ninja Dual Zone Air Fryer, ensuring they are standing upright and not touching each other.
7. Select Zone 1, choose the AIR FRY program, and set the temperature to 180°C. Set the time to 20-25 minutes. Select MATCH. Press the START/STOP button to begin cooking.
8. After 10-12 minutes of cooking, pause the air fryer, open it, and carefully rotate the bell peppers for even cooking.
9. Close the air fryer and resume cooking until the bell peppers are tender and the filling is heated through.
10. Once cooked, remove the **stuffed bell peppers** from air fryer and transfer them to a serving dish.

Quiche-Stuffed Peppers

Serves: 2 | Prep & Cook time: 35 Min

- 2 large bell peppers (red, yellow, or orange)
- 4 large eggs
- 100ml milk
- 75g shredded cheddar cheese
- 50g diced cooked ham
- 50g diced red onion
- 50g diced cherry tomatoes
- 1 tablespoon chopped fresh parsley
- Salt and pepper to taste.

DIRECTIONS:

1. Cut off the tops of the bell peppers and remove the seeds and membranes from the inside. Set aside.
2. In a bowl, whisk together the eggs and milk. Season with salt and pepper.
3. Add the shredded cheddar cheese, diced cooked ham, diced red onion, diced cherry tomatoes, and chopped fresh parsley to the egg mixture. Stir well to combine.
4. Place the bell peppers in basket of Zone 1.
5. Carefully pour the quiche mixture into each bell pepper, filling them about 3/4 full.
6. Place the air fryer basket in Zone 1 of the Ninja Dual Zone air fryer.
7. Select Zone 1, choose the AIR FRY function, and set the temperature to 180°C. Set the cooking time to 20 minutes (until the eggs are set and the tops are slightly golden). Press the START/STOP.
8. Once cooked, carefully remove the **Quiche-Stuffed Peppers** from Zone 1 using tongs or a spatula.
9. Allow them to cool for a few minutes before serving.

Chapter 8: Vegetarian Mains

Russet Potato Gratin

Serves: 6 | Prep & Cook time: 65 Min

- 1 kg Russet potatoes, peeled and thinly sliced
- 300 ml double cream
- 200 ml whole milk
- 150g shredded cheddar cheese
- 2 cloves garlic, minced
- 1 tablespoon fresh thyme leaves
- Salt and pepper to taste
- Butter for greasing.

DIRECTIONS:

1. Grease a baking dish with butter. Set it aside.
2. In a saucepan, heat the double cream, whole milk, minced garlic, and fresh thyme leaves over medium heat until hot but not boiling. Season with salt and pepper to taste.
3. Layer half of the sliced potatoes in the greased baking dish.
4. Pour half of the hot cream mixture over the potatoes, ensuring they are evenly coated.
5. Sprinkle half of the shredded cheddar cheese on top.
6. Layer the remaining sliced potatoes on top, followed by the remaining hot cream mixture.
7. Sprinkle the remaining shredded cheddar cheese over the top.
8. Place the baking dish in Zone 1. Select Zone 1, choose the AIR FRY, set the temperature to 180°C, cooking time to 45 minutes (until the potatoes are tender and the top is golden and bubbly). Press the START/STOP.
9. Once cooked, carefully remove the potato gratin from Zone 1 using oven mitts or tongs.
10. Allow **Russet Potato Gratin** to cool for a few minutes before serving.

Pesto Spinach Flatbread

Serves: 4 | Prep & Cook time: 25 Min

- 250g pre-made pizza dough (store-bought or homemade)
- 120g pesto sauce
- 50g baby spinach leaves
- 75g cherry tomatoes, halved
- 50g sliced red onion
- 100g shredded mozzarella cheese
- 25g grated Parmesan cheese
- 1/4 teaspoon dried oregano
- Salt and pepper to taste
- Olive oil for brushing.

DIRECTIONS:

1. On a lightly floured surface, roll out the pizza dough into a rectangular shape, about 1/4 inch thick.
2. Carefully transfer the rolled-out dough to basket of Zone 1.
3. Spread the pesto sauce evenly over the surface of the dough, leaving a small border around the edges.
4. Layer the baby spinach leaves, cherry tomatoes, and red onion slices over the pesto sauce.
5. Sprinkle the shredded mozzarella cheese and grated Parmesan cheese on top of the vegetables. Season with dried oregano, salt, and pepper to taste.
6. Place the air fryer basket in Zone 1. Select Zone 1, choose the AIR FRY, set the temperature to 200°C, cooking time to 10 minutes (until it turns golden brown and the cheese has melted). Press the START/STOP.
7. Once cooked, carefully remove the flatbread from Zone 1 using tongs or a spatula.
8. Brush the edges of the flatbread with olive oil for added flavor and shine.
9. Allow the **Pesto Spinach Flatbread** to cool for a few minutes, then cut it into desired portions and serve.

Stuffed Portobellos

Serves: 4 | Prep & Cook time: 30 Min

- 4 large Portobello mushrooms
- 200g fresh spinach
- 150g feta cheese, crumbled
- 1 red bell pepper, diced
- 1 small red onion, diced
- 2 cloves garlic, minced
- 2 tablespoons olive oil
- 1 teaspoon dried thyme
- Salt and pepper to taste.

DIRECTIONS:

1. Clean the Portobello mushrooms and remove the stems. Set them aside.
2. In a pan, heat 1 tablespoon of olive oil over medium heat. Add the diced red bell pepper, red onion, and minced garlic. Sauté until softened and fragrant.
3. Add the fresh spinach to the pan and cook until wilted. Season with salt, pepper, and dried thyme. Remove from heat and set aside.
4. In a separate bowl, crumble the feta cheese.
5. Brush the Portobello mushroom caps with the remaining olive oil. Place them in Zone 1 of the air fryer basket.
6. Fill each mushroom cap with the sautéed spinach mixture and top with crumbled feta cheese.
7. Select Zone 1, choose the AIR FRY, set the temperature to 180°C, cooking time to 15 minutes (until the mushrooms are tender and the cheese is melted and slightly golden.). Press the START/STOP.
8. Once cooked, carefully remove the **Stuffed Portobellos** from Zone 1 using tongs or a spatula.
9. Allow the stuffed mushrooms to cool for a few minutes before serving.

Cheese Stuffed Peppers

Serves: 2 | Prep & Cook time: 40 Min

- 2 large bell peppers (red, yellow, or orange)
- 100g cream cheese
- 50g grated cheddar cheese
- 2 tablespoons grated Parmesan cheese
- 1 tablespoon chopped fresh basil
- 1 tablespoon chopped fresh parsley
- 1/2 teaspoon garlic powder
- Salt and pepper to taste.

DIRECTIONS:

1. Cut off the tops of the bell peppers and remove the seeds and membranes from the inside. Set aside.
2. In a bowl, combine the cream cheese, grated cheddar cheese, grated Parmesan cheese, chopped fresh basil, chopped fresh parsley, garlic powder, salt, and pepper. Mix well to create a creamy filling.
3. Stuff each bell pepper with the cheese filling, ensuring they are evenly filled.
4. Place the stuffed peppers in basket of Zone 1. Select Zone 1, choose the AIR FRY function, and set the temperature to 180°C. Set the cooking time to 15 minutes (until the peppers are tender and the cheese filling is melted and slightly golden). Press the START/STOP button to begin cooking.
5. Once cooked, carefully remove the cheese stuffed peppers from Zone 1 using tongs or a spatula.
6. Allow the **Cheese Stuffed Peppers** to cool for a few minutes before serving.

Mediterranean Air Fried Veggies

Serves: 4 | Prep & Cook time: 25 Min

- 2 medium zucchini, sliced into rounds
- 1 large red bell pepper, sliced into strips
- 1 large yellow bell pepper, sliced into strips
- 1 red onion, cut into wedges
- 200g cherry tomatoes
- 2 tablespoons olive oil
- 2 cloves garlic, minced
- 1 teaspoon dried oregano
- 1 teaspoon dried basil
- Salt and pepper to taste
- Fresh parsley, for garnish.

DIRECTIONS:

1. In a large bowl, combine the sliced zucchini, red and yellow bell peppers, red onion wedges, cherry tomatoes, olive oil, minced garlic, dried oregano, dried basil, salt, and pepper. Toss well to coat the vegetables evenly with the seasonings and oil.
2. Select Zone 1, choose the AIR FRY program, and preheat the air fryer to 200°C
3. Place the seasoned vegetables in basket of Zone 1.
4. Select Zone 1, choose the AIR FRY function, and set the temperature to 200°C. Set the cooking time to 12 minutes. Press the START/STOP button to begin cooking.
5. Shaking the basket or stirring the veggies halfway through to ensure even cooking.
6. Once cooked, carefully remove the **Mediterranean Air Fried Veggies** from Zone 1 using tongs or a spatula.
7. Garnish with fresh parsley and serve as a side dish or as a topping for salads, wraps, or sandwiches.

Air-fried Radishes

Serves: 2 | Prep & Cook time: 20 Min

- 400g radishes, trimmed and halved
- 1 tablespoon olive oil
- 1 teaspoon garlic powder
- 1/2 teaspoon paprika
- Salt and pepper, to taste
- Fresh parsley or chives, chopped (for garnish, optional)

DIRECTIONS:

1. In a bowl, toss the radishes with olive oil, garlic powder, paprika, salt, and pepper until they are well coated.
2. Lightly grease Zone 1 of the air fryer with cooking spray or a small amount of oil.
3. Place the seasoned radishes in Zone 1 of the Ninja Dual Zone Air Fryer, making sure they are in a single layer and not overcrowded.
4. Select Zone 1, choose the AIR FRY program, and set the temperature to 200°C. Set the time to 12-15 minutes.
5. Press the START/STOP button to begin cooking.
6. After 6-8 minutes of cooking, pause the air fryer, open it, and shake or stir the radishes for even cooking.
7. Close the air fryer and resume cooking until the radishes are golden brown and tender, about 6-7 more minutes.
8. Once cooked, remove the **air-fried radishes** from air fryer and transfer them to a serving dish.
9. Garnish with fresh parsley or chives, if desired.

Stuffed Tomatoes

Serves: 4 | Prep & Cook time: 30 Min

- 4 large tomatoes
- 200g breadcrumbs
- 100g grated cheddar cheese
- 1 small onion, finely chopped
- 2 cloves of garlic, minced
- 1 tablespoon chopped fresh parsley
- 1 tablespoon chopped fresh basil
- Salt and pepper to taste
- Olive oil for drizzling.

DIRECTIONS:

1. Cut off the tops of the tomatoes and scoop out the pulp and seeds, creating a hollow cavity. Set aside the tomato shells.
2. In a mixing bowl, combine the breadcrumbs, grated cheddar cheese, chopped onion, minced garlic, parsley, basil, salt, and pepper. Mix well.
3. Fill each tomato shell with the breadcrumb mixture, pressing it gently to ensure it's tightly packed.
4. Place the stuffed tomatoes in Zone 1 of the air fryer, making sure they are stable and won't tip over.
5. Drizzle a little olive oil over the top of each stuffed tomato.
6. Select Zone 1, choose the BAKE program, and set the temperature to 180°C. Set the time to 15 minutes. Press START/STOP to begin cooking.
7. Once cooked, carefully remove the stuffed tomatoes from the air fryer using oven mitts or tongs.
8. Serve the **stuffed tomatoes** hot as a delicious side dish or light main course.

Curly Fries

Serves: 2 | Prep & Cook time: 35 Min

- 2 large potatoes
- 2 tablespoons vegetable oil
- 1 teaspoon paprika
- 1/2 teaspoon garlic powder
- 1/2 teaspoon onion powder
- 1/2 teaspoon dried oregano
- Salt and pepper to taste.

DIRECTIONS:

1. Peel the potatoes and wash them thoroughly.
2. Using a spiralizer or a vegetable peeler, cut the potatoes into curly or wavy fries.
3. In a large bowl, toss the curly fries with vegetable oil, paprika, garlic powder, onion powder, dried oregano, salt, and pepper. Make sure the fries are evenly coated with the seasoning.
4. Place the seasoned curly fries in both Zone of the air fryer, making sure they are spread out in a single layer.
5. Select Zone 1, choose the AIR FRY program, and set the temperature to 200°C. Set the time to 20 minutes. Select MATCH. Press START/STOP to begin cooking.
6. After 10 minutes of cooking, pause the air fryer, open it, and shake the basket or use tongs to flip the curly fries to ensure even cooking.
7. Close the air fryer and resume cooking for the remaining time or until the curly fries are golden brown and crispy.
8. Once cooked, carefully remove the curly fries from the air fryer using oven mitts or tongs.
9. Serve the **curly fries** hot as a delicious snack or side dish.

Herb & Lemon Cauliflower

Serves: 4 | Prep & Cook time: 30 Min

- 1 large cauliflower, cut into florets
- 3 tablespoons olive oil
- 2 tablespoons fresh lemon juice
- Zest of 1 lemon
- 2 cloves garlic, minced
- 1 teaspoon dried thyme
- 1 teaspoon dried rosemary
- Salt and pepper to taste
- Fresh parsley, chopped (for garnish)

DIRECTIONS:

1. In a large bowl, combine the olive oil, lemon juice, lemon zest, minced garlic, dried thyme, dried rosemary, salt, and pepper. Mix well.
2. Add the cauliflower florets to the bowl and toss them in the herb and lemon mixture until they are well coated.
3. Place the coated cauliflower florets in two zone of the air fryer, ensuring they are spread out in a single layer.
4. Select Zone 1, choose the AIR FRY program, and set the temperature to 200°C. Set the time to 20 minutes. Select MATCH. Press START/STOP to begin cooking.
5. After 10 minutes of cooking, pause the air fryer, open it, and shake the basket or use tongs to flip the cauliflower florets for even cooking.
6. Close the air fryer and resume cooking for the remaining time or until the cauliflower is tender and lightly browned.
7. Once cooked, carefully remove the herb and lemon cauliflower from the air fryer using oven mitts or tongs.
8. Garnish with fresh chopped parsley for added freshness and flavor.
9. Serve the **herb and lemon cauliflower** as a side dish or a delicious vegetarian main course.

Cheesy Cabbage Wedges

Serves: 4 | Prep & Cook time: 25 Min

- 1 medium green cabbage
- 4 tablespoons melted butter
- 1 teaspoon garlic powder
- 1 teaspoon paprika
- Salt and pepper to taste
- 100g grated cheddar cheese
- Fresh parsley, for garnish.

DIRECTIONS:

1. Cut the cabbage into quarters, leaving the core intact to hold the wedges together.
2. In a small bowl, combine the melted butter, garlic powder, paprika, salt, and pepper. Mix well.
3. Brush the melted butter mixture onto all sides of the cabbage wedges, ensuring they are evenly coated.
4. Place the seasoned cabbage wedges in Zone 1 of the air fryer.
5. Select Zone 1, choose the AIR FRY function, and set the temperature to 200°C. Set the cooking time to 15 minutes (until they are tender and lightly charred on the edges). Press the START/STOP.
6. Once cooked, carefully remove the cabbage wedges from Zone 1 using tongs or a spatula.
7. Sprinkle the grated cheddar cheese over the cabbage wedges, allowing it to melt slightly from the residual heat.
8. Garnish with fresh parsley. Enjoy **Cheesy Cabbage Wedges** !

NOTE: When place the seasoned cabbage wedges in Zone 1, if they are too crowded, put the rest in zone 2 and cook on both zones. Don't forget to Select MATCH to duplicate settings across both zones

Cauliflower Rice-Stuffed Peppers

Serves: 4 | Prep & Cook time: 35 Min

- 4 large bell peppers (red, yellow, or orange)
- 1 cauliflower head
- 1 tablespoon olive oil
- 1 small onion, diced
- 2 cloves garlic, minced
- 200g mushrooms, sliced
- 1 teaspoon dried oregano
- 1 teaspoon dried basil
- Salt and pepper to taste
- 100g grated cheddar cheese
- Fresh parsley, for garnish.

DIRECTIONS:

1. Cut off the tops of the bell peppers and remove the seeds and membranes from the inside. Set aside.
2. Cut the cauliflower into florets and place them in a food processor. Pulse until the cauliflower resembles rice-like grains.
3. In a large skillet, heat the olive oil over medium heat. Add the diced onion and minced garlic, and sauté until softened and fragrant. Add the sliced mushrooms to the skillet and cook until they are golden brown and tender.
4. Add the cauliflower rice, dried oregano, dried basil, salt, and pepper to the skillet. Cook for about 5 minutes, stirring occasionally, until the cauliflower rice is tender.
5. Spoon the cauliflower rice mixture into the bell peppers, dividing it evenly among them.
6. Place the stuffed peppers in Zone 1 of the air fryer.
7. Select Zone 1, choose the AIR FRY function, and set the temperature to 180°C, cooking time to 15 minutes (until the peppers are tender and slightly charred). Press the START/STOP.
8. Once cooked, carefully remove the stuffed peppers from Zone 1 using tongs or a spatula.
9. Sprinkle the grated cheddar cheese over the stuffed peppers, allowing it to melt slightly from the residual heat.
10. Enjoy **Cauliflower Rice-Stuffed Peppers** !

Zucchini With Stuffing

Serves: 4 | Prep & Cook time: 35 Min

- 4 medium zucchini
- 200g breadcrumbs
- 50g grated Parmesan cheese
- 1 small onion, finely chopped
- 2 cloves of garlic, minced
- 2 tablespoons fresh parsley, chopped
- 2 tablespoons fresh basil, chopped
- 2 tablespoons olive oil
- Salt and pepper to taste.

DIRECTIONS:

1. Cut the zucchini in half lengthwise and scoop out the flesh, leaving a hollow shell. Chop the zucchini flesh and set it aside.
2. In a bowl, combine the breadcrumbs, grated Parmesan cheese, chopped onion, minced garlic, parsley, basil, olive oil, salt, and pepper. Mix well to combine.
3. Add the chopped zucchini flesh to the breadcrumb mixture and stir until evenly incorporated.
4. Lightly grease two Zone of the air fryer with olive oil.
5. Stuff the hollowed zucchini shells with the breadcrumb mixture, pressing it firmly.
6. Place the stuffed zucchini in two Zone, making sure they are in a single layer and not touching each other.
7. Select Zone 1, choose the AIR FRY program, and set the temperature to 180°C. Set the time to 20 minutes. Select MATCH. Press START/STOP to begin cooking.
8. After 10 minutes of cooking, pause the air fryer, open it, and flip the zucchini to ensure even browning. Resume cooking for the remaining time or until the zucchini are tender and the topping is golden brown.
9. Once cooked, remove the **zucchini with stuffing** from the air fryer and serve them hot.

Mixed Air Fry Veggies

Serves: 2 | Prep & Cook time: 30 Min

- 200g baby potatoes, halved or quartered
- 200g carrots, peeled and sliced into sticks
- 200g courgette (zucchini), sliced into rounds
- 200g bell peppers, sliced into strips
- 2 tablespoons olive oil
- 1 teaspoon dried mixed herbs
- 1/2 teaspoon garlic powder
- 1/2 teaspoon onion powder
- 1/2 teaspoon paprika
- Salt and pepper to taste.

DIRECTIONS:

1. In a large bowl, combine the baby potatoes, carrots, courgette, and bell peppers.
2. Drizzle olive oil over the vegetables and sprinkle with dried mixed herbs, garlic powder, onion powder, paprika, salt, and pepper. Toss until the vegetables are evenly coated with the seasoning.
3. Lightly grease Zone 1 of the air fryer with cooking spray or a small amount of oil.
4. Place the seasoned vegetables in Zone 1 of the air fryer, ensuring they are in a single layer and not overlapping.
5. Select Zone 1, choose the AIR FRY program, and set the temperature to 200°C. Set the time to 15-20 minutes, depending on your desired level of crispness. Press START/STOP to begin cooking.
6. After 10 minutes of cooking, pause the air fryer, open it, and carefully toss the vegetables to ensure even cooking.
7. Close the air fryer and resume cooking for the remaining time or until the vegetables are tender and slightly crispy.
8. Once cooked, remove the **mixed air fry veggies** from the air fryer and serve hot as a side dish or as a main course.

Chickpea Fritters

Serves: 2 | Prep & Cook time: 30 Min

- 200g chickpeas, cooked and drained
- 1 small onion, finely chopped
- 2 cloves garlic, minced
- 1 teaspoon ground cumin
- 1 teaspoon ground coriander
- 1/2 teaspoon paprika
- 1/2 teaspoon salt
- 1/4 teaspoon black pepper
- 2 tablespoons chopped fresh parsley
- 2 tablespoons plain flour
- 1 tablespoon lemon juice
- 1 tablespoon olive oil

DIRECTIONS:

1. In a mixing bowl, mash the chickpeas using a fork or potato masher until they are partially mashed but still have some texture.
2. Add the finely chopped onion, minced garlic, ground cumin, ground coriander, paprika, salt, black pepper, chopped fresh parsley, plain flour, and lemon juice to the mashed chickpeas. Mix well until all the ingredients are combined.
3. Divide the mixture into 8 equal portions and shape each portion into a small patty or fritter shape.
4. Lightly grease both Zone of the air fryer with olive oil.
5. Place the chickpea fritters in two Zone, ensuring they are in a single layer and not touching each other.
6. Select Zone 1, choose the AIR FRY program, and set the temperature to 200°C. Set the time to 12-15 minutes. Select MATCH. Press START/STOP to begin cooking.
7. After 6-8 minutes of cooking, pause the air fryer, open it, and carefully flip the chickpea fritters for even cooking. Resume cooking for the remaining time or until the fritters are golden brown and crispy.
8. Once cooked, remove the **chickpea fritters** from the air fryer using oven mitts or tongs.
9. Serve the chickpea fritters hot as a delicious appetizer or as a filling for sandwiches or wraps.

Croutons

Serves: 4 | Prep & Cook time: 15 Min

- 4 slices of bread, preferably stale or slightly dry
- 2 tablespoons olive oil
- 1 teaspoon dried herbs (such as thyme, rosemary, or oregano)
- 1/2 teaspoon garlic powder
- Salt and pepper to taste.

DIRECTIONS:

1. Cut the bread slices into bite-sized cubes or desired crouton shape.
2. In a mixing bowl, combine the olive oil, dried herbs, garlic powder, salt, and pepper. Stir well to combine.
3. Add the bread cubes to the bowl and toss until they are well coated with the oil and herb mixture.
4. Lightly grease Zone 1 of the air fryer with olive oil.
5. Place the bread cubes in Zone 1, ensuring they are in a single layer and not overlapping.
6. Select Zone 1, choose the AIR FRY program, and set the temperature to 180°C. Set the time to 10 minutes. Press START/STOP to begin cooking.
7. After 5 minutes of cooking, pause the air fryer, open it, and give the croutons a gentle shake or stir to ensure even cooking.
8. Close the air fryer and resume cooking for the remaining time or until the croutons are golden brown and crispy.
9. Once cooked, remove the **croutons** from the air fryer and let them cool slightly before using them in salads, soups, or other dishes.

Buffalo Seitan With Crispy Zucchini Noodles

Serves: 2 | Prep & Cook time: 25 Min

For the Buffalo Seitan:

- 200g seitan, sliced into strips
- 2 tablespoons hot sauce
- 1 tablespoon vegetable oil
- 1 tablespoon soy sauce
- 1 tablespoon maple syrup
- 1/2 teaspoon garlic powder
- 1/2 teaspoon onion powder
- Salt and pepper, to taste

For the Crispy Zucchini Noodles:

- 2 medium zucchinis, spiralized or julienned
- 1 tablespoon olive oil
- 1/2 teaspoon paprika
- Salt and pepper, to taste

For Serving:

- Ranch or blue cheese dressing
- Fresh parsley or cilantro, chopped (for garnish, optional)

DIRECTIONS

1. Preheat your Ninja Dual Zone Air Fryer to 200°C (Zone 1).
2. In a bowl, combine hot sauce, vegetable oil, soy sauce, maple syrup, garlic powder, onion powder, salt, and pepper. Mix well.
3. Add the seitan strips to the bowl and toss until they are evenly coated in the buffalo sauce mixture.
4. Lightly grease Zone 1 of the air fryer with cooking spray or a small amount of oil.
5. Place the buffalo seitan strips in Zone 1 of the Ninja Dual Zone Air Fryer, making sure they are in a single layer and not touching each other.
6. Select Zone 1, choose the AIR FRY program, and set the temperature to 200°C. Set the time to 10-12 minutes. Press the START/STOP button to begin cooking.
7. While the seitan is cooking, prepare the crispy zucchini noodles. In a separate bowl, toss the spiralized or julienned zucchini with olive oil, paprika, salt, and pepper.
8. Lightly grease Zone 2 of the air fryer with cooking spray or a small amount of oil.
9. Place the seasoned zucchini noodles in Zone 2 of the Ninja Dual Zone Air Fryer, making sure they are in a single layer. Select Zone 2, choose the AIR CRISP program at a temperature of 200°C for 5-7 minutes. Press the START/STOP button to begin cooking.
10. Once the seitan has cooked for about 5 minutes, pause the air fryer, open it, and carefully flip the seitan strips in Zone 1 for even cooking (about 5-7 more minutes)
11. Once cooked, remove the buffalo seitan from Zone 1 and the crispy zucchini noodles from Zone 2 of the air fryer.
12. Serve the buffalo seitan on top of the crispy zucchini noodles. Drizzle with ranch or blue cheese dressing and garnish with fresh parsley or cilantro, if desired.
13. Enjoy the delicious and spicy **Buffalo Seitan with Crispy Zucchini Noodles** as a satisfying and flavorful meal!

Super Vegetable Burger

Serves: 8 | Prep & Cook time: 30 Min

- 400g canned chickpeas, drained and rinsed
- 200g canned black beans, drained and rinsed
- 200g cooked quinoa
- 100g grated carrots
- 100g grated zucchini
- 100g chopped mushrooms
- 50g diced red onion
- 2 cloves garlic, minced
- 50g breadcrumbs
- 2 tablespoons chopped fresh parsley
- 1 teaspoon ground cumin
- 1 teaspoon paprika
- Salt and pepper to taste
- Burger buns and toppings of your choice (lettuce, tomato, onion, etc.)

DIRECTIONS

1. Select Zone 1, choose the AIR FRY program, and preheat the air fryer to 200°C. Select MATCH to duplicate settings across both zones.
2. In a large bowl, mash the chickpeas and black beans with a fork or potato masher until chunky.
3. Add the cooked quinoa, grated carrots, grated zucchini, chopped mushrooms, diced red onion, minced garlic, breadcrumbs, chopped fresh parsley, ground cumin, paprika, salt, and pepper to the bowl. Mix well to combine all the ingredients.
4. Shape the mixture into 8 equal-sized patties, pressing them firmly to hold their shape.
5. Evenly dividing and place the vegetable patties in two zone of the air fryer basket.
6. Select Zone 1, choose the AIR FRY, and set the temperature to 200°C. Set the time to 15 minutes. Select MATCH. Press the START/STOP.
7. Flipping them halfway through, until they are golden brown and crispy.
8. Once cooked, carefully remove the vegetable burgers using a spatula.
9. Serve the **Super Vegetable Burgers** on burger buns with your choice of toppings, such as lettuce, tomato, and onion.

Baked Brazilian Pineapple

Serves: 4 | Prep & Cook time: 20 Min

- 1 pineapple
- 2 tablespoons unsalted butter, melted
- 2 tablespoons honey
- 1 teaspoon ground cinnamon
- Juice of 1 lime

DIRECTIONS:

1. In Zone 1 of the Ninja Dual Zone air fryer, select the BAKE function and preheat it to 180°C.
2. Peel and core the pineapple, and cut it into thick slices or wedges.
3. In a small bowl, mix together the melted butter, honey, ground cinnamon, and lime juice.
4. Brush the pineapple slices with the honey-butter mixture, making sure to coat them evenly.
5. Place the pineapple slices in Zone 1 of the air fryer in a single layer.
6. Choose BAKE, and set the temperature to 180°C, cooking time to 12 minutes (until the pineapple is golden brown and caramelized). Press the START/STOP. Turning once halfway through the cooking time.
7. Once baked, carefully remove the pineapple slices from the Ninja Dual Zone air fryer and transfer them to a serving platter.
8. Serve the **Baked Brazilian Pineapple** slices as a delicious dessert or a side dish.

Chapter 9: Desserts

Mini Cheesecake

Serves: 2 | Prep & Cook time: 30 Min

- 150g digestive biscuits
- 50g unsalted butter, melted
- 200g cream cheese
- 60g caster sugar
- 1/2 teaspoon vanilla extract
- 1 egg
- Fresh berries, for garnish (optional)

DIRECTIONS:

1. Crush the digestive biscuits into fine crumbs. This can be done by placing them in a sealable plastic bag and crushing them with a rolling pin or by using a food processor.
2. In a bowl, mix the melted butter with the digestive biscuit crumbs until well combined.
3. Divide the biscuit mixture equally between two small ramekins or oven-safe dishes. Press the mixture down firmly to form the cheesecake crust.
4. In a separate bowl, beat the cream cheese, caster sugar, and vanilla extract until smooth and creamy.
5. Add the egg to the cream cheese mixture and beat until well incorporated.
6. Pour the cream cheese mixture over the prepared biscuit crust in each ramekin, filling them almost to the top. Place the ramekins in Zone 1 of the air fryer, select the BAKE, temperature to 160°C, cooking time to 15 minutes (until the cheesecakes are set and slightly golden around the edges)
7. Once baked, carefully remove the ramekins from the Ninja Dual Zone air fryer and let the mini cheesecakes cool to room temperature.
8. Once cooled, refrigerate the mini cheesecakes for at least 2 hours or until chilled and firm. You can garnish the **mini cheesecakes** with fresh berries, if desired.

Gingerbread | Makes 1 loaf

Serves: 4 | Prep & Cook time: 50 Min

- 225g plain flour
- 1 teaspoon ground ginger
- 1 teaspoon ground cinnamon
- 1/2 teaspoon ground nutmeg
- 1/2 teaspoon baking soda
- 1/4 teaspoon salt
- 115g unsalted butter, softened
- 115g light brown sugar
- 2 large eggs
- 4 tablespoons golden syrup
- 120ml whole milk.

DIRECTIONS:

1. In a mixing bowl, whisk together the plain flour, ground ginger, ground cinnamon, ground nutmeg, baking soda, and salt until well combined.
2. In a separate large mixing bowl, cream together the softened butter and light brown sugar until light and fluffy.
3. Add the eggs to the butter mixture, one at a time, beating well after each addition. Stir in the golden syrup.
4. Gradually add the dry ingredient mixture to the wet mixture, alternating with the whole milk. Mix until just combined, being careful not to overmix.
5. Grease and line a loaf pan that fits in Zone 1 of the air fryer.
6. Pour the gingerbread batter into the prepared loaf pan.
7. Place the loaf pan in Zone 1. Select Zone 1, choose BAKE, and set the temperature to 200°C. Set the cooking time to 35 minutes (until a toothpick inserted into the center comes out clean). Press the START/STOP.
8. Once baked, carefully remove the loaf pan from the air fryer and allow the gingerbread to cool in the pan for a few minutes before transferring it to a wire rack to cool completely.
9. Once cooled, slice and serve the **gingerbread** as desired.

White Chocolate Cookies | Makes 10 cookies

Serves: 4 | Prep & Cook time: 25 Min

- 115g unsalted butter, softened
- 100g light brown sugar
- 100g granulated sugar
- 1 large egg
- 1 teaspoon vanilla extract
- 225g plain flour
- 1/2 teaspoon baking soda
- 1/4 teaspoon salt
- 150g white chocolate chips.

DIRECTIONS:

1. In a large mixing bowl, cream together the softened butter, light brown sugar, and granulated sugar until light and fluffy.
2. Add the egg and vanilla extract to the butter mixture. Beat well until fully incorporated.
3. In a separate bowl, whisk together the plain flour, baking soda, and salt.
4. Gradually add the dry ingredient mixture to the wet mixture, mixing until just combined.
5. Fold in the white chocolate chips until evenly distributed throughout the cookie dough.
6. In Zone 1 of the Ninja Dual Zone air fryer, select the BAKE function and preheat it to 180°C in few minutes.
7. Roll the cookie dough into approximately 10 equal-sized balls and place them on a baking sheet that fits in Zone 1 of the air fryer.
8. Place the baking sheet in Zone 1 of the air fryer. Choose BAKE, and set the temperature to 180°C, cooking time to 12 minutes (until the cookies are golden brown around the edges). Press the START/STOP.
9. Once baked, carefully remove the baking sheet from the air fryer and allow the cookies to cool for a few minutes on the sheet before transferring them to a wire rack to cool completely.
10. Once cooled, serve and enjoy the delicious **White Chocolate Cookies**.

Pumpkin Pudding with Vanilla Wafers

Serves: 4 | Prep & Cook time: 30 Min

- 400g canned pumpkin puree
- 200ml double cream
- 100g light brown sugar
- 2 large eggs
- 1 teaspoon vanilla extract
- 1 teaspoon pumpkin pie spice
- A pinch of salt
- 16 vanilla wafers
- Whipped cream, for serving (optional)
- Ground cinnamon, for garnish (optional)

DIRECTIONS:

1. In a mixing bowl, combine the pumpkin puree, double cream, light brown sugar, eggs, vanilla extract, pumpkin pie spice, and salt. Whisk together until well combined and smooth.
2. Grease 4 individual ramekins or oven-safe dishes.
3. Place 4 vanilla wafers at the bottom of each greased ramekin.
4. Pour the pumpkin pudding mixture over the vanilla wafers, dividing it equally among the ramekins.
5. Place the filled ramekins in Zone 1. Select the BAKE function and set the temperature to 180°C. Set the cooking time to 20 minutes and press the START/STOP button to begin baking.
6. Once the cooking time is complete, carefully remove the ramekins from the air fryer using oven mitts or tongs.
7. Allow the **pumpkin pudding** to cool to room temperature, then refrigerate for at least 2 hours to chill and set.
8. Just before serving, garnish with a dollop of whipped cream and a sprinkle of ground cinnamon, if desired.

Blueberry Cheesecake Pies

Serves: 4 | Prep & Cook time: 40 Min

- 1kg cooking apples (such as Bramley), peeled, cored, and chopped
- 150g light brown sugar
- 1 teaspoon ground cinnamon
- 1/2 teaspoon ground nutmeg
- 1/4 teaspoon ground cloves
- Juice of 1 lemon
- 1/2 teaspoon vanilla extract.

DIRECTIONS:

1. Toss the blueberries with the maple syrup in a bowl. In a separate bowl, mix the soft cheese, vanilla and caster sugar.
2. Unroll the pastry and use a knife to cut the sheet into 4 equal rectangles. Brush the edges of each rectangle with a little beaten egg.
3. Divide the blueberries between the pastry, arranging them to one side of the rectangles and leaving a clear 1.5cm border around the edge. Place a spoonful of the soft cheese mixture on top of the blueberries.
4. Fold the pastry over like a book and press down the edges around the blueberries. Crimp the edges with a fork to seal the pastry, then brush the tops all over with beaten egg. Sprinkle each with 1/2 teaspoon demerara sugar. With a skewer, pierce two holes in the top of each pie.
5. Place 2 pies in zone 1, then insert drawer in unit. Place the other 2 pies in zone 2.
6. Select zone 1, select BAKE, set temperature to 180°C and set time to 15 minutes. Select MATCH. Press the START/STOP button to begin cooking.
7. When zones 1 and zone 2 time reaches 5 minutes, remove drawers from unit and turn the pies using silicone-tipped tongs. Reinsert drawer to continue cooking.
8. When cooking is complete, remove the pastries from drawers and cool on a wire rack for 10 minutes before serving.

Pumpkin Cookie with Cream Cheese Frosting

Serves: 6 | Prep & Cook time: 30 Min

For the cookies:

- 150g plain flour
- 1/2 teaspoon baking powder
- 1/2 teaspoon ground cinnamon
- 1/4 teaspoon ground nutmeg
- 1/4 teaspoon ground ginger
- 1/4 teaspoon salt
- 60g unsalted butter, softened
- 100g light brown sugar
- 100g pumpkin puree
- 1 large egg
- 1/2 teaspoon vanilla extract

For the cream cheese frosting:

- 60g cream cheese, softened
- 30g unsalted butter, softened
- 150g icing sugar
- 1/2 teaspoon vanilla extract.

DIRECTIONS

1. In Zone 1 of the Ninja Dual Zone air fryer, select the BAKE function and preheat it to 180°C.
2. In a mixing bowl, whisk together the plain flour, baking powder, ground cinnamon, ground nutmeg, ground ginger, and salt until well combined.
3. In a separate large mixing bowl, cream together the softened butter and light brown sugar until light and fluffy.
4. Add the pumpkin puree, egg, and vanilla extract to the butter mixture. Mix until well incorporated.
5. Gradually add the dry ingredient mixture to the wet mixture, mixing until just combined.
6. Drop spoonfuls of the cookie dough onto a baking sheet or in a baking pan that fits in Zone 1 of the air fryer.
7. Place the baking sheet or pan in Zone 1 of the air fryer.
8. Choose BAKE, and set the temperature to 180°C, cooking time to 12 minutes (until the cookies are set and slightly golden around the edges). Press the START/STOP.
9. Once baked, carefully remove the baking sheet or pan from the Ninja Dual Zone air fryer and allow the cookies to cool completely on a wire rack.
10. While the cookies are cooling, prepare the cream cheese frosting. In a mixing bowl, beat together the softened cream cheese, softened butter, icing sugar, and vanilla extract until smooth and creamy.
11. Once the cookies have cooled, spread or pipe the cream cheese frosting onto each cookie.
12. Serve and enjoy the delicious **Pumpkin Cookies with Cream Cheese Frosting**.

Chocolate Donuts

Serves: 4 | Prep & Cook time: 25 Min

- 200g all-purpose flour
- 40g cocoa powder
- 100g granulated sugar
- 2 teaspoons baking powder
- 1/4 teaspoon salt
- 150ml milk
- 2 tablespoons vegetable oil
- 1 teaspoon vanilla extract
- 1 large egg
- 50g chocolate chips (optional)
- Icing sugar for dusting (optional)

DIRECTIONS:

1. In a mixing bowl, combine the all-purpose flour, cocoa powder, granulated sugar, baking powder, and salt. Mix well to ensure even distribution of ingredients.
2. In a separate bowl, whisk together the milk, vegetable oil, vanilla extract, and egg until well combined.
3. Pour the wet ingredients into the dry ingredients and stir until just combined. Be careful not to overmix; a few lumps are fine. If desired, fold in the chocolate chips.
4. Preheat the Ninja Dual Zone Air Fryer to 180°C (both Zone). Lightly grease both Zone with cooking spray or a small amount of oil.
5. Spoon the batter into a piping bag or a resealable plastic bag with a corner snipped off.
6. Pipe the batter into the donut molds in two Zone of the air fryer, filling each mold about 2/3 full.
7. Select Zone 1, choose the AIR FRY program, and set the temperature to 180°C. Set the time to 8-10 minutes. Select MATCH. Press START/STOP to begin cooking.
8. After the cooking time, insert a toothpick into one of the donuts to check for doneness. If it comes out clean, the donuts are ready. If not, cook for an additional 2-3 minutes.
9. Once cooked, remove the chocolate donuts from the air fryer and let them cool slightly before removing them from the molds.
10. Dust the **donuts** with icing sugar, if desired, before serving.

Almond Butter Cookies | Serves 12 cookies

Serves: 4 | Prep & Cook time: 25 Min

- 100g almond butter
- 75g granulated sugar
- 40g unsalted butter, softened
- 1 large egg
- 1/2 teaspoon vanilla extract
- 100g all-purpose flour
- 1/2 teaspoon baking powder
- Pinch of salt
- 12 whole almonds (optional)

DIRECTIONS:

1. In a mixing bowl, cream together the almond butter, granulated sugar, and softened butter until well combined and creamy.
2. Add the egg and vanilla extract to the bowl and mix until fully incorporated.
3. In a separate bowl, whisk together the all-purpose flour, baking powder, and salt.
4. Gradually add the dry ingredients to the wet ingredients, mixing until a dough forms. The dough should be soft but not sticky. If the dough is too sticky, add a little more flour.
5. Divide the dough into 12 equal portions and roll each portion into a ball.
6. Preheat the Ninja Dual Zone Air Fryer to 180°C (both Zone). Lightly grease both Zone with cooking spray or a small amount of oil.
7. Place the cookie dough balls on two Zone, spacing them apart to allow for spreading.
8. If desired, press a whole almond onto the top of each cookie dough ball.
9. Select Zone 1, choose the AIR FRY program, and set the temperature to 180°C. Set the time to 8-10 minutes. Select MATCH. Press START/STOP to begin cooking.
10. After the cooking time, check the cookies for doneness. They should be golden brown around the edges.
11. Once cooked, remove the **almond butter cookies** from the air fryer and let them cool on a wire rack before serving.

Apple Dutch Baby

Serves: 4 | Prep & Cook time: 35 Min

- 2 medium apples, peeled, cored, and sliced
- 2 tablespoons unsalted butter
- 3 large eggs
- 120ml whole milk
- 70g all-purpose flour
- 2 tablespoons granulated sugar
- 1/2 teaspoon vanilla extract
- 1/4 teaspoon ground cinnamon
- Pinch of salt
- Powdered sugar, for dusting
- Maple syrup or honey, for serving

DIRECTIONS:

1. In a skillet or frying pan, melt the butter over medium heat. Add the sliced apples and cook until they are tender and lightly caramelized, about 5 minutes. Set aside.
2. In a mixing bowl, whisk together the eggs, milk, flour, granulated sugar, vanilla extract, ground cinnamon, and salt until smooth and well combined.
3. Grease a round baking dish or oven-safe skillet and pour the batter into it.
4. Arrange the cooked apple slices on top of the batter.
5. Place the baking dish or skillet in Zone 1, Choose BAKE, and set the temperature to 200°C, cooking time to 20 minutes (until the Dutch Baby is puffed up and golden brown). Press the START/STOP.
6. Once cooked, carefully remove the baking dish or skillet from the Ninja Dual Zone air fryer. The Dutch Baby will deflate slightly as it cools.
7. Dust the Apple Dutch Baby with powdered sugar.
8. Serve the **Apple Dutch Baby** warm, cut into wedges, and drizzle with maple syrup or honey.

Ricotta Lemon Poppy Seed Cake

Serves: 4 | Prep & Cook time: 45 Min

- 125g ricotta cheese
- 100g unsalted butter, softened
- 150g granulated sugar
- 2 large eggs
- Zest of 1 lemon
- Juice of 1/2 lemon
- 1 teaspoon vanilla extract
- 150g all-purpose flour
- 1 teaspoon baking powder
- 1 tablespoon poppy seeds
- Pinch of salt
- Icing sugar, for dusting.

DIRECTIONS:

1. In a mixing bowl, combine the ricotta cheese, softened butter, and granulated sugar. Mix until creamy and well combined.
2. Add the eggs, lemon zest, lemon juice, and vanilla extract to the bowl. Mix until smooth.
3. In a separate bowl, whisk together the all-purpose flour, baking powder, poppy seeds, and salt.
4. Gradually add the dry ingredients to the wet ingredients and mix until just combined. Avoid overmixing.
5. Grease a round baking pan that fits in the air fryer basket and pour the cake batter into it.
6. Place the baking pan in Zone 1 of the air fryer, choose BAKE, and set the temperature to 160°C, cooking time to 30 minutes (until a toothpick inserted into the center comes out clean). Press the START/STOP.
7. Once cooked, carefully remove the baking pan from the Ninja Dual Zone air fryer and let the cake cool in the pan for a few minutes.
8. Transfer the cake to a wire rack to cool completely.
9. Dust the **Ricotta Lemon Poppy Seed Cake** with icing sugar before serving.

Jelly Doughnuts

Serves: 4 | Prep & Cook time: 55 Min

- 250g all-purpose flour
- 50g granulated sugar
- 1 teaspoon instant yeast
- 1/4 teaspoon salt
- 120ml warm milk
- 1 large egg
- 2 tablespoons unsalted butter, melted
- Vegetable oil for frying
- 4 tablespoons strawberry or raspberry jam
- Icing sugar for dusting (optional)

DIRECTIONS

1. In a mixing bowl, combine the all-purpose flour, granulated sugar, instant yeast, and salt. Mix well.
2. In a separate bowl, whisk together the warm milk, egg, and melted butter.
3. Pour the wet ingredients into the dry ingredients and mix until a soft dough forms.
4. Turn the dough out onto a lightly floured surface and knead for about 5 minutes until smooth and elastic. Divide the dough into 8 equal portions and shape each portion into a ball.
5. Place the dough balls on a lightly greased tray, cover with a clean kitchen towel, and let them rise for about 30 minutes until doubled in size.
6. Lightly grease the air fryer basket or the rack in Zone 1 with vegetable oil.
7. Preheat your Ninja Dual Zone Air Fryer to 180°C.
8. Place 4 dough balls in each Zone of the Ninja Dual Zone Air Fryer, making sure they are not touching each other.
9. Select Zone 1, choose the AIR FRY program, and set the temperature to 180°C. Set the time to 10-12 minutes. Select MATCH to duplicate settings across both zones.
10. Press the START/STOP button to begin cooking.
11. Flip the doughnuts halfway through the cooking time to ensure even browning.
12. Once cooked, carefully remove the doughnuts from the air fryer and let them cool for a few minutes.
13. Fill a piping bag fitted with a small round tip with the strawberry or raspberry jam.
14. Insert the tip of the piping bag into each doughnut and gently squeeze to fill it with jam.
15. Dust the **Jelly Doughnuts** with icing sugar, if desired, before serving.

Printed in Great Britain
by Amazon

34210285R00068